Mandate Politics

Whether or not voters consciously use their votes to send messages about their preferences for public policy, the Washington community sometimes comes to believe that it has heard such a message. In this book, the authors ask, "What then happens?" This book focuses on these perceived mandates – where they come from and how they alter the behaviors of members of Congress, the media, and voters.

These events are rare. Only three elections in postwar America (1964, 1980, and 1994) were declared mandates by media consensus. These declarations, however, had a profound if ephemeral impact on members of Congress. They altered the fundamental gridlock that prevents Congress from adopting major policy changes. The responses by members of Congress to these three elections are responsible for many of the defining policies of this era. Despite their infrequency, then, mandates are important to the face of public policy and our understanding of Congress, the president, and the responsiveness of our government more generally.

Lawrence J. Grossback is Adjunct Assistant Research Professor in the Department of Political Science at West Virginia University and works as a policy analyst for the federal government. He has published articles in the *American Journal of Political Science; British Journal of Political Science; Journal of Health Policy, Politics, and Law; American Politics Research;* and other journals and edited volumes. He was co-winner of the 2002 Patrick J. Fett Award from the Midwest Political Science Association for the best paper on Congress and the Presidency.

David A. M. Peterson is Associate Professor of Political Science at Texas A&M University. His work has been supported by the National Science Foundation and has appeared in the *American Journal of Political Science, Journal of Politics, Political Behavior,* and other journals. He was co-winner of the 2002 Patrick J. Fett Award from the Midwest Political Science Association for the best paper on Congress and the Presidency.

James A. Stimson is Raymond Dawson Distinguished Bicentennial Professor of Political Science at the University of North Carolina at Chapel Hill. He has authored or coauthored five books: *Yeas and Nays: Normal Decision-Making in the U.S. House of Representatives* (with Donald R. Matthews); *Issue Evolution: Race and the Reconstruction of American Politics* (with Edward G. Carmines); *Public Opinion in America: Moods, Cycles, and Swings; The Macro Polity* (with Robert S. Erikson and Michael B. MacKuen); and *Tides of Consent: How Public Opinion Shapes American Politics.* He has won the Heinz Eulau and Gladys Kammerer Awards of the American Political Science Association, the Chastain Award of the Southern Political Science Association, and the Pi Sigma Alpha Award of the Midwest Political Science Association.

Mandate Politics

LAWRENCE J. GROSSBACK
West Virginia University

DAVID A. M. PETERSON
Texas A&M University

JAMES A. STIMSON
University of North Carolina, Chapel Hill

CAMBRIDGE
UNIVERSITY PRESS

CAMBRIDGE UNIVERSITY PRESS
Cambridge, New York, Melbourne, Madrid, Cape Town, Singapore, São Paulo

Cambridge University Press
32 Avenue of the Americas, New York, NY 10013-2473, USA

www.cambridge.org
Information on this title: www.cambridge.org/9780521866545

First published 2006

Printed in the United States of America

A catalog record for this publication is available from the British Library.

Library of Congress Cataloging in Publication Data

Grossback, Lawrence James.
Mandate politics / Lawrence J. Grossback, David A. M. Peterson, James A. Stimson.
p. cm.
Includes bibliographical references and index.
ISBN-13: 978-0-521-86654-5 (hardback)
ISBN-10: 0-521-86654-5 (hardback)
1. Political planning – United States. 2. Elections – United States.
3. Representative government and representation – United States.
I. Peterson, David A. M., 1973– II. Stimson, James A. III. Title.
JK468.P64G76 2006
324.973 – dc22   20060011095

ISBN-13   978-0-521-86654-5 hardback
ISBN-10   0-521-86654-5 hardback

Contents

List of Figures

List of Tables

Preface

We confess. We are sinners. According to the gospel of political methodology, one should never let method determine choice of topics to investigate. The prohibition is so sensible that it needs no explanation. And yet this is exactly what we did. In the spring of 1997, four of us sat around a table in a seminar room in Minneapolis and asked the question, "What would be a good application of the duration modeling techniques that we had been studying together?"

In a few minutes of conversation, we spun a story about observing members of Congress faced with a Washington consensus that the election just passed had carried a voter mandate. We asked what the reaction should look like and, because this was a methods course and we are social scientists, how we could model it. Although we may not have known it then, the question of the impact of perceived mandates had been investigated before. Importantly, however, the tools used and assumptions made were blunt. Scholars asked if the year following a mandate was different from the year that preceded it, concluding that it was not. The duration model, in contrast, focused on a temporary response that had run its course, as we now know, by midyear – and lost most of its force well before that. In this case, the tool matters.

The question originated from both the 1994 election and its aftermath, on the one hand, and the opportunity to test a piece of the theory Stimson had developed elsewhere ("Dynamic Representation," with coauthors Michael B. MacKuen and Robert S. Erikson), on the other.

The four of us were quite amazed at the dynamics of the aftermath of the Republican revolution. The Republicans took control of Congress for the first time in a generation and were poised to make tremendous changes in public policy. In the space of two years, this opportunity had collapsed. We could not agree if there really was something in public opinion that propelled the Republicans to power in 1994. We could not agree if that election had been a mandate or if *any* election could be a mandate. Despite years of trying, we never could develop a test of whether or not a mandate had occurred. Instead, we decided that the beliefs of the members of Congress comprised a more testable, and ultimately more theoretically interesting, question.

The second motivation is the one we were more interested in and the one that maintained this project for eight years. Stimson's work in "Dynamic Representation" proposed a theory that members of Congress were forward-looking observers of public opinion who constantly monitored all the signs of what the public wanted and how that might be changing so that they could be ahead of the curve, reacting to what could be known today so that they would never be caught out of line with public sentiment in a future election. This required members to be ambitious – and they are – and to be assiduous processors of all the little scraps of information that might forecast where the public was heading. If these were true, then the currents that move elections should be fully anticipated and the elections themselves should have no influence on the future behavior of members. Future elections in this world of rational expectations might move current behavior, but past elections were just history.

But we found one detail in this story troublesome. In a world of uncertainty, it should be the case that even the most assiduous information processors make forecast errors. Trying very hard to get it right, as if one's whole career depends on it – which it does – still does not guarantee that all will be foreseen. The loose end is the answer to the question, "What if some elections surprise, their outcome different from what informed observers expected?" Then, contrary to the main line of the dynamic representation theory, these elections should matter. Surprises do lead rational actors to change behavior.

And so our interest in statistical theory, tied to our observations about politics and grafted onto a nugget of theoretical anomaly, led to an animated discussion of thirty minutes or so in which much of the research that would eventually lead to this book was anticipated. It played out in our minds without a scrap of data at hand.

We were a class, not a research group. We were not looking for a project and had no plan to do something together. In most circumstances it would have been a fun discussion and then . . . nothing, on to the next week's topic. The work we anticipated was massive and none of it had been started. There was no assurance that it would work, that we actually could demonstrate that mandate elections changed behavior. It was crucial in this regard that the computer routines that produced the data for the dynamic representation research were available off the shelf. With them in hand, we generated the aggregate voting patterns that will be seen in Chapter 4, a matter of a few hours' work. This evidence was unmistakable. For the three elections that we considered reasonable candidates to have been perceived by Washington insiders as mandates, there was noticeable movement toward the mandate at the beginning of a new Congress, which then decayed back to normal voting patterns as the session progressed – exactly what we had anticipated with our prior theory.

From that first discussion in which we had real results, tentative though they were, we were hooked. We knew then that the difficult and sensitive duration analysis was likely to uncover the same patterns already seen in the easy aggregate analyses. It was worth the effort, which was considerable. We ceased to be a class and became a research team of four. Our fourth member, Amy Gangl, was present at the creation and made valuable contributions to our early research program, including the first published article from it. To our regret, she decided that this project was too far removed from the political psychology that is her specialty and professional identity.

And what of the duration modeling that sparked the discussion that was the origin of this research? Well, we did it. As we thought it would be in advance, it became the key evidence for the micro theory of member response to mandates. But to put the matter in context, it is just one section in one chapter of the seven-chapter book that follows. How members of Congress respond to news of a mandate is a pretty important part of our story, but it led us to ask several other questions. How do the media create the story of an election being a mandate? Why do some elections create these messages, whereas others don't? What are the policy changes induced by these responses? How do voters react to these responses in subsequent elections? Each of these questions was completely beyond our original plan and each caused us to immerse ourselves in history and in textual analysis that were well beyond our normal research styles. In combination, we have a more or less complete story of mandate elections that begins with those elections and ends when members of Congress face the voters two years later.

For eight years, we immersed ourselves in the idea of electoral mandates. This book is the result.

Acknowledgments

As with any other book, the authors leaned heavily on many other people. The project began while all three of us were at the University of Minnesota. Minnesota provided a rich academic environment and strong research support to launch this effort. We all have since moved on and have received institutional support from the University of North Carolina at Chapel Hill (Stimson), Texas A&M University (Peterson), and West Virginia University (Grossback). WVU, in particular, awarded a Faculty Senate Research Grant to assist in this project.

Several of our friends and colleagues have provided valuable comments on portions of the manuscript. These include Patricia Hurley, Kim Hill, B. Dan Wood, Eric Lawrence, Paul Kellstedt, Walter Mebane, Adam Berinsky, Mike MacKuen, Jan Leighley, Stephen Ansolabehere, Neal Beck, Scott Chrichlow, Stephen Borelli, Byron Schaeffer, participants of the 1997 and 1998 Annual Meetings of the Society for the Study of Political Methodology, and the WVU Department of Political Science Research Seminar. Janet Box-Steffensmeier and Brad Jones, in particular, helped with the duration analysis and encouraged the project along the way. Chaun Stores, Teresa Hutchins, and Brian Fogarty provided invaluable research assistance. Brian deserves special mention for his work on the content analysis in Chapter 2.

Some of our data come from archival sources. The Inter-University Consortium for Political and Social Research provided much of the roll call and election data we rely on. We are indebted to Keith Poole for his meticulous work archiving and making public roll call data for recent congresses. Data on key laws were taken from David Mayhew, and we appreciate his continued efforts at identifying these laws and making the data public.

We also thank Lori Biederman, Dianne Stimson, and Teresa Warkel. Each of us in our own way knows why.

Finally, this project began with four authors. When we started exploring mandates, Amy Gangl was an equal partner. At some point, Amy decided that this project did not fit into her research agenda and chose to work on other things. She helped develop the theory and analysis that form the basis of Chapter 3 of this book (and the *American Journal of Political Science* article that was an earlier version of that chapter). Several of the ideas that we would explore after she was no longer part of the project, particularly those about the media in Chapter 2, were heavily influenced by our early discussions with her on the topic. We know that this book is better off because of her involvement at the beginning – and worse off for her absence at the end.

A Single Time in a Single Place

On the morning of November 5, 1964, Arthur Krock of the *New York Times* posed a problem for newly elected President Lyndon Johnson. How would he answer the "great question created by the most emphatic vote of preference ever given to a national candidate: How will he use the mandate to lead and govern that has been so overwhelmingly tendered by the American people?" (1964, p. 44). Krock's words capture the reaction of many to the landslide that had brought victory to more than Johnson. In the upcoming Congress, the Democrats would hold a two to one margin in both chambers. Thirty-eight new House Democrats extended their majority to 295 seats while two new Democratic Senators gave them a total of 68, the second largest majority the Democrats had ever held in both chambers (Morris 1965). If there ever was a partisan surge, this was it.

There was, as always, a debate over whether the Democratic surge constituted a mandate for Johnson's policies. Most Republicans attributed the defeat to the rejection of Barry Goldwater's brand of conservatism. Some Democrats argued that the victory was rooted more broadly in support of liberalism than in support of Johnson. There was some truth to this last notion. Outside the South, liberal Democrats replaced conservative Republicans. In the South, conservative Republicans replaced equally conservative Democrats. The liberal gains thus went beyond additional Democratic seats. Still, many in the media and in politics saw this as a mandate, and many of them ranked it as among the most significant in history. Even reluctant Republicans had to concede defeat and admit that voters had expressed their support for the major parts of Johnson's program. One Republican congressman summed up the meaning of the election well. "He's got the votes. There's not much we can do to stop his program if we tried" ("Great Society" Editorial, p. E1).

Johnson's answer to Krock's question came the following January in his State of the Union Address. Johnson (1965a) would seek the creation of a "Great Society [that] asks not how much, but how good; not only how to create wealth but how to use it; not only how fast we are going, but where we are headed." The Great Society included calls for health insurance for the elderly, the federal funds to support secondary and higher education, a department of housing and urban development to lead a war on poverty, and efforts to fight crime and disease. Johnson also touched on his desire to build on the passage of the Civil Rights Act the year before. The statement was brief, promising "the elimination of barriers to voting rights," but it would come to have major consequence for American politics.

Voting rights were on the agenda of others as well, and well they should have been. In 1964, only about 43 percent of Southern blacks were registered to vote, but the figure was as low as 7 percent in Mississippi (Davidson 1994). One week after the Democratic landslide, the Southern Christian Leadership Conference decided that it needed a rallying point around which to build support for voting rights across the nation (Davidson 1992). The rallying point would be Selma, Alabama. Selma and surrounding Dallas County had 30,000 blacks eligible to vote, of whom only 355 were then registered. Soon the Rev. Martin Luther King Jr. would request a meeting with the president to discuss voting rights proposals. The election results played a role in the renewed drive to pass a voting rights bill. One reporter noted that "passage of the Civil Rights Act of 1964 and the outcome of the Nov. 3 election had the effect of crumbling much of the massive white opposition to change that existed in the Deep South states" (Herbers 1965, p. E5). It did not crush all the resistance, and it had little effect on the white leaders of Selma. It was they who on March 7, 1965 – hence forth known as "Bloody Sunday" – led a group of men on to Edmund Pettus Bridge to attack civil rights marchers, wounding close to a hundred.

The violence of Bloody Sunday led members of Congress from both parties to call on the Johnson administration to quickly send the anticipated voting rights bill to Congress. The mandate made it time to act. Johnson had wide public support outside the South, and he saw the need to take advantage of the Democrats' massive advantage in Congress before Southern support for the party eroded further (Davidson 1994). On March 15, the president spoke to the country about the need for a voting rights bill. He spoke of an American promise that had to be kept and of the destiny of democracy. He also spoke of Selma. His words were eloquent:

...at times history and fate meet at a single time in a single place to shape a turning point in man's unending search for freedom. So it was at Lexington and Concord. So it was a century ago at Appomattox. So it was last week in Selma, Alabama. (Johnson 1965b)

As critical as Selma was, it was not enough to ensure passage of a forceful voting rights bill. The bill had to get through the U.S. Senate where Southerners controlled key committees and where they could filibuster the bill to death. The first challenge was the Senate Judiciary Committee. Since 1953, James Eastland (D-MS) had chaired the committee. In that time, 122 civil rights bills had been referred to the committee. Of that number, only one was ever reported back, and that case required the entire Senate to overrule the chair (Kenworthy 1965a). The mandate consensus, however, had strengthened Johnson's hand and the hand of the Senate leadership. To get past Senator Eastland, the Senate leadership required that the bill be reported back in fifteen days. If not, the party leaders would cancel the Easter recess. The mandate effect also lowered the threat of a filibuster. A number of Southern Senators who had opposed the Civil Rights Act of 1964 appeared ready to allow a bill to come to a vote. Their ranks included J. W. Fulbright of Arkansas, George Smathers of Florida, and Albert Gore of Tennessee. Of them, only Gore would join four other Southern Senators who – along with sixty-five others – would vote for cloture.

The belief in a mandate would have a direct influence on the content of the bill as well. In analyses to come, we suggest that certain elections, such as 1964, are perceived to carry a message about the will of the voters. These mandates lead members of Congress to reevaluate how

to vote on legislation to satisfy their constituents. We can assess the
effect of the perceived mandate by asking what would the outcome of
roll call votes have been absent these reevaluations. We rerun history
(by a method to be detailed later) to observe roll call outcomes in a
"normal" 1965 Senate – one in which the effect of the mandate has
been removed.

Absent the mandate, two votes on amendments to the Voting Rights
Act would have come out differently. One was a (Republican) amendment to limit the ability of the U.S. Attorney General to bring cases
under the Act's provisions. The second was a Southern Democratic
amendment that would have given federal courts in the South the dis-
cretion to hear cases arising from the Act. Both had a simple purpose:
gutting the enforcement provisions of the Act. By putting enforcement
in the hands of Southern state attorneys general and sitting Southern
judges, the amendments would have watered the bill down to almost
nothing, an endorsement of voting rights that would be without practi-
cal effect. Both were defeated, primarily because the spirit of the times
led a small number of Senators to cast votes that were more liberal
than would have been the case in normal conditions.

The result was a second "single time in a single place" when history
and fate met to extend freedom to a long oppressed group of citizens.
The moment came on August 6, 1965, in the U.S. Capitol. President
Johnson entered the President's Room off the Senate chamber, the very
same room that Abraham Lincoln entered in 1861 to free slaves pressed
into confederate military duty. He sat at the desk he used as a Senator and at which some believe Lincoln also sat on that earlier day
(Kenworthy 1965b). There Lincoln freed the slaves, and there Johnson
signed the Voting Rights Act of 1965. Johnson (1965c, p. 8) would
remark that "today is a triumph for freedom as huge as any victory
that's ever been won on any battlefield."

The implication here is striking. The Democratic gains in Congress
were not enough to ensure an effective voting rights bill.[1] Absent the
unusual politics a sense of mandate put in place, the Great Society
would have been very different, especially to black voters across the

---

[1] And we don't need to rerun history to know that numbers weren't enough. That *same*
89th Senate would turn balky the following year, denying Johnson much of what he
wanted.

South. Mississippi may not have seen the percentage of blacks registered to vote increase from 7 percent in 1964 to nearly 60 percent in 1968. Nor would the South see the number of black elected officials rise from fewer than 100 to over 3,265 by 1989 (Davidson 1992). Absent the mandate, the history of racial politics and, indeed, partisan politics might have been very different (Carmines and Stimson 1989).

1.0.1 "Our Enemy is Time" – Budget Politics and the Reagan Revolution

On May 7, 1981, two roll call votes took place in the House of Representatives. The first sought to replace the Fiscal 1982 Budget Resolution prepared by the (Democratic) majority Leadership with a substitute resolution written by Ronald Reagan's budget director, David Stockman. The second would be on the adoption of the resolution that emerged. The substitute resolution was the Reagan revolution. It called for nearly $37 billion in spending cuts for fiscal 1982, another $44 billion in cuts by fiscal 1984, and left room for a 30 percent cut in individual tax rates that would cost nearly $50 billion in its first year and over $700 billion over five years. The goal was simple; fundamentally scale back the scope of the federal government. Victory for Reagan was not assured. The Republicans had 192 members in the House, 26 short of a majority.

In scheduling the two votes, the Democratic controlled Rules Committee had imposed an up or down vote on the revolution. The Reagan White House framed the vote in simple terms (Stockman 1986, p. 174): "Are you with Ronald Reagan or against him?" In the end, 253 members were with Reagan on the first vote, 270 on the second. Sixty-three Democrats joined 190 Republicans to defeat the Democratic alternative. As members prepared to vote on final adoption, the easy victory led Minority Leader Robert Michel (R-IL) to proclaim, "Let history show that we provided the margin of difference that changed the course of American government" (*CQ Almanac* 1981, p. 253).

Six months earlier, in October 1980, historic change in the course of American government was not inevitable, in fact, it seemed unlikely. Opinion polls showed that President Jimmy Carter had eroded the lead Ronald Reagan had held since early summer (Pomper 1981). Just before the two candidates debated on October 28, Carter opened a narrow lead. The revolution was in jeopardy. For a number of reasons, Carter's lead did not hold. Reagan won a majority of the popular vote (51.7 percent, a ten-point margin), and dominated the Electoral College, winning nearly 91 percent of the votes.

Because the election was expected to be tight, Reagan's victory surprised few. A solid debate performance and a final embarrassment of Carter by the Iranian government allowed Reagan to regain his lead in the polls a week out from the election. The extent of the victory, however, "*did* surprise nearly everyone," and "real surprise, indeed astonishment" came in the congressional elections (Jacob 1981, p. 119, emphasis original). The newly elected 97th Congress would see the exit of twelve incumbent Democratic Senators (many among the most liberal), Republican control of the Senate for the first time in twenty-eight years, and a Republican gain of thirty-three seats in the House. Mandate or not, the election was a clear victory for the Republican Party.

The shift in Congress caught the attention of many. On election night, future Reagan Budget Director David Stockman's wrote that his "eyes remained fixed on the House and Senate races across the nation" (1986, p. 69). Congress was of great concern to him because Republicans "needed a substantial transfusion of conservative blood. Otherwise, the world's greatest parliamentary institution would grind the revolution to a halt, presidential mandate or not." The conservatives got just what they needed. David Broder (1980, p. A1) captured the consensus well: "voters ... elected the most conservative Congress in a generation. Their action strengthened the president-elect's right to interpret his victory as a mandate for the policies of stronger defense and skimpier government." Conservatives believed that control of the Senate gave the mandate claim an institutional component that made it credible (Fenno 1991). The mandate interpretation did not escape the Republican Senators who would lead the revolution in their chamber. Budget Committee Chair Pete Domenici (R-NM) remarked, "There is an American mandate ... the size of the budget cannot grow as fast" (Fenno 1991, p. 50). The mandate perception did not escape the Democrats either. House Speaker Tip O'Neill admitted that "some of the old ways have to change. It's a new day. A different time" (Stockman 1986, p. 121).

The surprising victory margin, the widely shared mandate perception, and the Republican surge in Congress set the stage for the budget showdown on May 7. The budget became the legislative embodiment of the mandate. Domenici made that clear to the Senate: "The blueprint contained in this resolution is clear. It is unequivocal. It responds directly to the mandate of the American people and the requests of our President" (*CQ Almanac* 1981, p. 247). The timing of the showdown, just four months after Reagan's inauguration, stemmed directly from the recognition that the effect of the mandate might be transient.

Almost immediately, the Reagan team saw the need to move quickly. Stockman made speed a central element of the budget strategy by beginning his first strategy memo with "Our enemy is time" (Stockman 1986, p. 76). He feared "the resurgent political forces of the status quo." He feared the inevitable change in political information flowing to members of Congress. His fear produced a plan that would see the release of the Reagan budget by mid-February, and a final budget resolution by mid-May. The Republican forces knew that they had to demonstrate their ability to govern and do so quickly. To do so, they married speed with a deft procedural innovation. They would pass budget reconciliation bills first in order to give the entire Reagan package the force of law while avoiding the long deliberations and inevitable alterations that would come if they took the normal path of first passing nonbinding resolutions.

The dramatic Republican surge in Congress offered the final element of a strategy rooted in mandate politics. The revolution would begin in the Senate. Control of the Senate offered the opportunity to use the new majority to push the budget through the Senate and then use it as leverage against the House (Rattner 1981; Fenno 1991). The strategy worked, but not without its share of setbacks. The initial budget package was defeated in committee when three Republicans voted with Democrats because they thought the budget abandoned the principle of a balanced budget. Victory came after an additional $44 billion in unspecified future budget cuts was included. The changes were superficial, but they succeeded in winning back the three Republicans and three Southern Democrats (*CQ Almanac* 1981). It didn't hurt that President Reagan had lobbied members from a hospital bed where he was recovering from a would-be assassin's bullet.

A recovering Reagan also played a crucial role in the House. There, the strategy focused on assembling a coalition of Republicans and conservative Southern Democrats, called Boll-Weevils, to get the votes for

the budget. Stockman (1986, p. 173) clearly believed that members
were engaging in representation by responding to the electorate's signal. He noted that by the time of the House vote on the budget they
could count on enough Boll-Weevils because after the assassination
attempt Reagan's "already imposing strength in the Boll-Weevils' districts had reached never-before-recorded levels." Stockman was right.
Reagan's lobbying proved effective. He equated his budget with the
will of the people, a signal few in Congress could afford not to acknowledge. Reagan's efforts prompted Tip O'Neill to concede defeat:
"I can read [members of] Congress. They go with the will of the people,
and the will of the people is to go along with the president" (Dewar
1981).

In the end, Reagan would have to compromise in the House. A
slightly revised budget with smaller deficit numbers passed the House
with the support of eighty-four of O'Neill's Democrats. Republican
gains in Congress were not enough to pass the bill that would guide
the revolution, nor was Democratic control of the House enough to
defeat it. As we will demonstrate later, the victory was the result of
members voting more conservatively than we would expect under normal conditions. Absent the mandate effect, many of the Democrats
and a few Republicans would not have voted to support the revolution. They took the mandate consensus as a signal of public opinion
and voted to protect themselves in the 1982 election.

The erosion of that consensus ensured that the final budget enacted
by Congress did not contain all of the elements of the resolution passed
on May 7. But it would contain most of what Reagan wanted. Close
to $38 billion in spending cuts became law, cuts that would total $52
billion by 1986, a 9 percent reduction in the federal budget. The budget
cut food stamps, child nutrition programs, rent supports, Aid to Fami-
lies with Dependent Children, student loans, and some Social Security
benefits. By one calculation, the budget cut $12 billion from Great So-
ciety grants and services by 1986, a 25 percent cut in the welfare state
(Stockman 1986).

Stockman was right to see time as the revolution's enemy. Not long
after the final budget victories in late June, the sense of mandate began to unravel. During the August recess, many members of Congress
received "a dose of constituency reaction" that included the idea that
the social spending cuts had gone too far (Fenno 1991, p. 58). The

media, too, would sense the change and switch its tone to suggesting that the mandate was overinterpreted. Reagan would eventually be forced to raise taxes and make additional cuts to deal with a ballooning deficit; mandate politics would give way to politics as usual. The policy changes were already in place. The Great Society had been scaled back, taxes lowered, and a decade of deficit politics lay ahead.

1.0.2 "We Heard America Shouting" – The End of Welfare as We Know It

In January 1995, President Bill Clinton stepped into the House Chamber to deliver his third State of the Union Address. It had been nearly fifteen years since the Reagan mandate had scaled back the welfare state, and it was now evident that a second round of changes was at hand. The president admitted as much in his speech. He summed up the recent midterm election, noting that "... we didn't hear America singing, we heard America shouting" (Clinton 1995). It was clear from his speech that the president thought the shouts were a call to change how Washington worked. In an attempt to downplay the Republican victory, he interpreted the meaning of the election as a renewal of the call for change that helped drive his victory in 1992. "We must agree that the American people certainly voted for change in 1992 and 1994," he said. But the election of 1992 was not at all like that of 1994.

President Clinton's explanation fell on deaf ears. By the time of his speech the idea that the 1994 elections were driven by an anti-incumbent mood had been dismissed by the Washington community. It is easy to see why. The Republicans gained fifty-two seats in the House, assuming control of the chamber for the time since 1952, a feat reminiscent of their taking control of the Senate in 1980. A loss of fifty seats by the president's party is not unheard of; conventional wisdom sees midterm elections as a referendum on the sitting president, but something happened in 1994 that made this election different. Not a single Republican incumbent – Senate, House, or gubernatorial – lost. All 177 survived. Democratic incumbents fared much worse. In the House, thirty-five Republican challengers beat incumbent Democrats. In the Senate, Republicans challengers beat three incumbent Democrats and won all six open Democratic seats. The day after the election Senator

Richard Shelby of Alabama switched parties to give the Republicans a nine-seat gain. The magnitude of the victory led David Broder (1994, p. A1) to acknowledge that "The center of power in American politics moved sharply rightward yesterday." The damage to the Democrats went further. Broder noted that "voters gave the GOP an expanded mandate to govern by its own principles" by defeating five incumbent Democratic governors, reelecting Republican governors in California, Illinois, Michigan, and Ohio, and by giving Republicans control of statehouses in New York, Pennsylvania, and Texas. Call it what you want – a landslide, a sea change, realignment, or a revolution – this was no mere call for change.

Mandate interpretations cannot be based on mere claims; they require palpable evidence of change in the electorate. The election of 1994 offered such evidence, but a mandate consensus was not inevitable. A number of competing explanations arose. Democrats, in a clear effort of damage control, placed the blame on anti-incumbent feelings and the Clinton administration's failings on health care reform, gays in the military, and civil rights. Political scientists, too, downplayed the idea of a mandate. They saw little change in the partisan or ideological makeup of the electorate and too diverse a group of issues at play to signal major change. What they saw was a partisan victory rooted in standard midterm losses, an unfocused antigovernment mood, Republican gains in the South, and a strong mobilization effort by conservative groups (Wilcox 1995). They also discounted the importance of the now famous "Contract with America." The Contract was the Republican's vehicle to nationalize the effort to gain control of the House by uniting their candidates behind a set of clear conservative principles and proposals. Skeptics cited as evidence polls that found that fewer than 20 percent of the public had heard of the Contract, only one in four of those planning to vote Republican knew of it, and fewer than 5 percent of voters approved of it (Wilcox 1995, p. 21).

These interpretations were not the view that pervaded Washington in the run up to the president's speech. The deans of the Washington pundit community weighed in heavily in favor of a conservative Republican mandate. David Broder (1994, p. A1) called it "A historic Republican triumph fueled more by ideology than anti-incumbency." Richard Wolf (1994, p. 1A), writing on the front page of *USA Today*, called it a "romp to the right," "a Republican revolution of historic proportions," and added "at least for now they have a mandate."Charles Krauthammer (1994, p. A31) argued that Republicans "gratuitously decided to advance an ideological program and seek an ideological mandate," and that the result was an "epochal political change." William Safire (1994, p. A17) echoed this sentiment, noting that Newt Gingrich had nationalized the local elections, shifted the "center of power in domestic affairs," and was now "keeper of the voters' mandate." Safire also coined a new word, "disentitlementarianism." This, he argued, was the "hard part" of the new Republican mandate – welfare reform. Where the Reagan revolution sought to scale back the welfare state, the Gingrich revolution sought to do away with it all together by ending the sixty-year-old entitlement to unlimited welfare benefits. This was not the original goal of the Contract. The welfare plank did not call for an end to the existing entitlement program, but the conservative tide swept even the Republican victors farther to the right.

Bill Clinton put welfare reform on the national agenda during the 1992 campaign by calling for an "end to welfare as we know it." The Republican mandate and the "Contract with America" not only took over the national agenda from Clinton but also drastically altered the course of welfare reform. President Clinton's 1994 proposal required that after two years of benefits AFDC recipients would have to work to continue receiving benefits. To help facilitate the transition from welfare to work, the proposal sought an additional $9.3 billion for job training and child care assistance. Welfare reform languished on the national agenda, taking a back seat to health care, until the Contract put a Republican version on the fast track. The Republican version pushed far more dramatic changes, more conservative than those in the Contract. It sought to end the entitlement by putting a lifetime limit on benefits, it transferred most power to the states by turning welfare into a block grant, and some versions sought to reduce funding by limiting benefits to families who have new children, unwed mothers, immigrants, and some disabled children. The shift in the agenda led one journalist to note that "many liberals seem downright stunned by how fast the debate over welfare reform has moved to the right" (Toner 1995, p. A22). Representative Charles Rangel (D-NY) summed up the liberal position well, noting that "Two years ago, I thought my biggest fight would be against Clinton's proposals" (Toner 1995, p. A22).

The Republican success forced President Clinton to try to reassert his relevance in the welfare debate (and in national governance in general), but he dropped his proposal all together, perhaps realizing that electoral conditions necessitated that he work with congressional Republicans. During the 104th Congress, the president did not ask anyone to reintroduce his welfare bill and no one ever did (Pear 1995). He ceded near total control of the debate to the Republican leadership and was forced to rely on Democrats and moderate Republicans in the Senate to forestall a complete Republican victory. Recognizing the transient nature of their mandate, and the ability to set the tone for upcoming negotiations, House Republicans moved to quickly pass a bill within the first 100 days of the new Congress. The House bill sought $62 billion in cuts over five years by shifting most benefits to block grants, imposing strict time limits for benefits, imposing a cap on benefits to families to discourage out of wedlock births, denying cash benefits to unwed teen mothers, most legal immigrants, drug addicts, and alcoholics. By moving quickly, Republican leaders in the House were able to capitalize on the mandate perception by forcing a Democratic president to the sidelines and presenting the more moderate Senate with a very conservative bill that would set the tone for the conference committee negotiations.

The sense of mandate went beyond shifting the terms of the debate; it contributed directly to the final passage of the House bill and the content of the Senate bill that went to conference. The Republican leadership in the House pushed a welfare reform bill through the House on March 24. For the most part, it was a partisan affair, with only nine Democrats voting for the bill. Without the sense of conservative mandate in Washington, however, passage of the bill would not have been so easy and its contents surely would have been more compromised. Mandate politics came into play when the House considered the rule for floor debate. The rule allowed consideration of 31 amendments out of more than 150 proposed. It excluded most of the contentious ones, including several proposed by Republicans who were strongly antiabortion.

The antiabortion members raised concerns that the bill would promote abortions by penalizing unwed teenage mothers and awarding states for reducing their out of wedlock birthrate. This group of conservative Republicans wanted to liberalize the bill by allowing unwed teenage mothers to receive welfare checks through guardians or to pay for baby supplies and housing. A bare majority of 217 voted for the rule, which allowed the leadership bill to come to a vote. Absent the sense of mandate, the rule would have failed and the leadership would have been forced to accept votes on far more amendments. With it, the House passed the most conservative version of the bill.

The Senate would have a moderating effect, with the moderation increasing as the mandate perception eroded over time. The Senate would not act until mid-September, and although the final bill chipped away at the conservative edges of what the House had passed, the core reform of ending the welfare entitlement remained. Even nine months into the year, belief in mandate still led to a more conservative bill. One vote stands out. Conservative Democratic Senator John Breaux (LA) proposed an amendment that would have imposed a penalty on states that did not continue to spend 90 percent of their fiscal 1994 total on welfare. This was an attempt to ensure that states would not gut their own programs when they took control of the new federal block grant programs. The House required no specific spending level; states were free to spend as much, or as little, as they chose. The Breaux amendment was defeated, eventually replaced with a 75 percent requirement pushed by moderate Republicans.

It would take until August 1996 for welfare reform to become law, but not before Republican leaders sought to end the Medicaid entitlement along with it. In the end, they would settle for a compromise between the House and Senate bills of 1995, bills that ended welfare as we knew it, but on Republican terms. Washington had indeed heard America shouting and responded with the most dramatic reversal of the welfare state since the Reagan revolution. The election had given Republicans the majorities in Congress to seek major change. The sense of mandate that flowed from the election produced the impetus to do it.

There is a common element in the three stories of politics we have told. It is that politicians behave differently when they come to the belief that a recent election has signaled a voter mandate. Also in common is the idea that these changes in behavior are highly consequential for the essential outcomes of government. Important things happen, that is, not only from the election itself but also from the *interpretation* of what it meant. We are in need of a theory that comprehends how interpreting an election outcome can in and of itself produce changes in behavior and outcomes. That is where we turn.

1.1 MANDATES AS SOCIAL CONSTRUCTIONS

The idea of voter mandate has two facets. One is that voters consciously use their votes to send a signal to government about their preferences. We have an immense literature on that issue that tends, on balance, to be dismissive of it. The second is that public officials receive the signal – and then act on it. It is this second piece that is the focus of this book.

We have no particular interest in whether voters consciously signal their preferences. Indeed, it does not matter to us whether or not they do. Politicians do sometimes *believe* that voters have sent a message. They tell us so in their words and, more important, in their deeds. Much evidence of that is to come. This belief is a social construction, a shared conclusion that derives from the public interaction over the interpretation of an election. A shared conclusion is a will of the wisp kind of reality, not tangible like percentage of the vote or seats won and lost. But undeniably humans do act on beliefs. And so beliefs about the political world – whether or not they are correct – do matter.

Electoral mandates might be real or might be merely misperceptions, social constructions of an election outcome that install a message never in the minds of voters. Perceptions of mandate do occur; that is a simple matter of fact. Whether those perceptions reflect reality we leave open for the moment.

The mandate in either case is a message about voter preferences for policy change. We ask here what to expect of the impact of that message. To answer the question we need a theory that gives context to these particular messages. We wish to explain why political actors (members of the U.S. Congress, for example) respond to the message. To do so, we begin with the micro decision model of dynamic representation (Stimson, MacKuen, and Erikson 1995).

We assume that politicians have preferences over policy choices and also that they seek to be reelected. Their situation in general is that particular issues are likely to present them with some options that are expedient for the reelection goal and others which better satisfy their preferences. Confronting a sequence of such tough choices, they develop a strategy for dealing with them. On issues that present themselves on the main left-right division of American politics this strategy becomes a normal trade-off between where they would prefer to be and where electoral concern forces them to be. In the typical situation, in which professional politician preferences are more thoughtful, consistent, and intense than those of the amateur electorate, that means that politicians will typically compromise between a more extreme preferred position and a more moderate expedient one. This trade-off between safety and electoral security can be thought of as an equilibrium choice strategy, what politicians would do if there were no particular information flow about the issue at hand that would move them from their normal positions.

Politicians care about elections yet to be held. And career politicians would be wise to think beyond just the next one. Information that might leverage their difficult trade-off decisions would of course be valued. But such information is scarce. The problem is that public views are not crystallized about issue specifics and there is great uncertainty about which issues will shape the future electoral agenda. Thus, politicians have a considerable need for information of a generic sort – specific information has a very high likelihood of being irrelevant to the electoral future – that can guide their ongoing decisions. They acquire mountains of information from the buzz of politics, the inside the beltway conversations that constitute the professional life of national politics. This might be systematic as in poll results but also might be the shared reflections of professionals in face to face conversations, all intensely concerned with tracking the public pulse.

Politicians attend to the conversations, make inferences about the public mood, and use those inferences to update their decision strategy. Of particular importance is information about movements in general tendencies, "Mood" in the Stimson (1991, 1998) formulation. Information about general movements in public preference give one some ability to forecast future elections. In this view, the most expedient position is variable over time, not constant. It depends on where public views are going. Thus, the equilibrium choice strategy is also dynamic; the trade-off point shifts as estimates of where the public stands change.

Thus, we expect politicians in the aggregate to shift with public opinion. Where professional politicians concur on the direction of change in public attitudes, then the shift in individual positions will be unidirectional. And a shift wholly (or at least largely) in the same direction will shift outcomes. The distribution of politicians will respond to the public opinion signal. Thus current public opinion, acted on by politicians anticipating future elections, shifts political choices.

What of the elections themselves, what signal do they provide? In the rational expectations view to which we subscribe, events that can be forecasted convey no information when the forecasts prove to be accurate. Only surprises, the difference between forecast and actual outcome, matter. Only surprises convey information. Thus, elections, to the extent that their outcomes are expected, provide no signal to politicians for how they should choose differently.

Politicians in this formulation project likely election outcomes from uncertain information about public preferences. Ambition dictates that they should try hard and that they should do it well. But uncertainty is inherent. A public that is usually tuned out of politics becomes hard to predict on the rare occasions when it tunes in. Thus, no matter how hard they try and no matter what skill and knowledge they bring to the issue, professional politicians will sometimes be surprised by election outcomes. These will be the elections declared to be mandates. When the confident expectations of professional observers are notably wrong, then observers begin to search for a message that can explain the unexpected.

On relatively rare occasions, the arbiters of American politics – politicians, who are not particularly credible, and media commentators who are – decide that an election carries a message. When they do so, then all who seek election must rethink their beliefs about the electoral future. Mandates have potential influence, therefore, because they lead political actors to recalculate their strategies. Those on the winning side are emboldened to recalibrate their positions in the direction of their true preferences. Those on the losing side are threatened by future defeat and pressed to move toward the "message" for electoral security.

In the rational anticipation model of Stimson, MacKuen, and Erikson (1995) politicians think only about the future, ignoring elections past. Here we depart by noting that mandate elections provide (or appear to provide) information as well. When elections turn out as most expect, then beliefs about the lay of the political land are confirmed. When they deviate markedly and observers find a message in the deviation, then strategy must be revised and positions rethought.

Thus, the central idea of mandates in our theory is that they carry information about the political future that causes calculating politicians to change their anticipations. The mandates that we study always turn out to be perceived mandates, views about a change in fundamental political orientations that are eventually discounted and disconfirmed by new information. Thus, the expected effect is transient, a shift of beliefs and positions that eventually decays back to an equilibrium little different from the preelection period. However illusory the perceptions and however transient the effects, important political actions occur under the impetus of the mandate and they become established facts in law, which are neither illusory nor transient.

1.2 THE STUDY OF MANDATES

The three stories with which we began illustrate how three separate mandate perceptions changed politics and public policy. They hint at a larger story of mandate politics, a story unlike those previously told in political science. Existing work on electoral mandates is unable to explain these episodes. The existing institutional work tends to focus on presidents. The behavioral work focuses on the ability of the electorate to send a decisive policy signal, often deprecating it. Nothing in our literature focuses much on the processes that link voters and election outcomes to the behavior of representatives. Our theory of electoral mandates naturally builds on what this literature has to say, so that is where we begin.

Like many people in political science, those who focus on institutions and those who study behavior are sometimes at cross-purposes. So it is in the case of mandates. Those who see mandates from the governance perspective – from inside the beltway – take a different view than those who focus on the voters. We take up these literatures in order.

1.2.1 Institutional Perspectives

Mandates, viewed as policy directives sent from electorates to governing elites, have long been an important aspect of the evaluation of democratic electoral systems. The translation of the electorate's preferences into governance and policy is central to most conceptualizations of representation. Shugart and Carey (1992) link policy mandates to two qualities of electoral systems: identifiability and efficiency. Identifiability refers to the voters' ability to identify competing potential governments and the policy differences that distinguish them. Efficiency refers to the extent that election results or voter intentions are translated directly into policy. In Shugart and Carey's (1992) view mandates are realistic only in proportional representation systems where a vote for a member of parliament translates directly into a clear choice for an executive government and a slate of legislation that the majority party will have the power to enact. Mandates, accordingly, are unlikely to emerge in presidential systems.

The winner-take-all system of American politics regularly results in disproportionate representation because the party winning the presidency controls the entire executive government, no matter the victory margin. Shugart and Carey (1992) argue that presidential systems are likely to produce a false sense of a mandate because the winner governs in a majoritarian manner while often having received the support of a minority of the electorate.

Despite these difficulties, observers of American politics have focused their attention (inappropriately we believe) on the existence of presidential mandates. Dahl (1990) traces the origins of the theory of presidential mandates to Woodrow Wilson's belief that the president is the only national voice, because he is the only one elected by the nation as a whole. Dahl (1990, p. 360) noted that "it has become commonplace for presidents and commentators alike to argue that by virtue of his election the president has received a mandate for his aims and policies from the people of the United States." The assumption underlying this view is that national elections carry messages about electoral preferences that are clear enough to serve as a directive to the president and to all other representatives as well.

Dahl (1990) and Kelley (1983) argue that the classic theory of presidential mandates is more myth than reality. Looking beyond the election returns to survey research, Kelley (1983) finds little evidence of widespread support for the specific policies advocated by many presidential winners, including those who won by the proverbial landslide.

Weinbaum and Judd (1970) look directly at how members of Congress perceive and react to mandates. Their study of congressional roll call votes after the 1964 and 1936 elections finds some evidence in support of a "mandated Congress," but they note that similar results can be found after every election. Their conclusion is that the key to presidential success after mandates comes from changes in the composition in the Congress, not from members of Congress changing their views or votes.

Although Dahl and Kelley found little in election returns and surveys to validate the classic mandate theory and Weinbaum and Judd find little support for members of Congress responding to real mandates, others cite contested electoral meanings and institutional conflict. Edwards (1989) began a reassessment of mandates by noting that what matters is the perception of a mandate and not the existence of a true policy directive sent by the electorate. Edwards (1989) also shifted the discussion away from the focus on presidents to a more party-centric view of mandates. This change came as a result of his interest in executive-legislative relations and the influence of the separation of powers on national policy making.

Jones (1999) takes a similar party-centric view, identifying mandates as election outcomes that put in place the elements of a responsible party model. In spite of the realities of separated institutions of government, Jones sees the responsible party model dominating postelection political commentary and press coverage. Mandates are instances in which election returns and postelection commentary reflect the conditions necessary for responsible party government: a clear ideological difference between the candidates; significant issues debated; a landslide presidential victory; and an accompanying party victory that sees the winner's party gain in Congress in a greater than expected fashion (Jones 1999).

Such an election provides a rational basis for declaring a mandate and sparks short-term electoral interpretation that includes use of the mandate idea. The main policy implication is that such elections produce agenda congruity across institutions – an agreement among major policy actors as to the general orientation of the policy problems to be addressed and the specific policy alternatives to be implemented. Jones agrees that mandates are more perception than reality, and that future information often raises questions about the strength of the mandate. But Congress and the president often act, he notes, before the mandate perception erodes.

Jones (1999) believes that the president makes strategic use of the mandate interpretation and that the perception of a mandate can induce Congress to concur with the president's agenda. Mandates are

instances in which there is enough agreement among actors to reduce the bargaining tension between the two major policy-making
institutions. Without such agreement, the chances of major policy
change are reduced and policy becomes a function of the outcome
of more contested negotiations between the president and Congress.

Conley (2001) emphasizes the president's strategic use of the mandate claim. She argues that presidents interpret election outcomes in an
effort to set the national policy agenda. For the president, the question
is, what does the outcome signify? Has the election provided enough of
a base of support to seek large-scale policy change? The president may
or may not link his or her electoral victory to a policy initiative. The
main impact of the election is that its interpretation can be exploited
to capitalize on a political opportunity.

Policy change, for Conley, is a function of the president first claiming a mandate and Congress then agreeing with him. If the position
of Congress is close to the claimed mandate and public opinion supports the president, then Congress will capitulate and enact policies
that reflect the mandate. She finds that presidents usually (but not
always) declare a mandate, and that when Congress agrees with the
president, or when the president fights it with public opinion, the president achieves more policy success. A mandates is thus a strategic tool
employed by the president to push the presidential agenda through
Congress.

The return to a focus on presidential mandates leaves us with a
literature that is not far from where it began. Mandates are no longer
seen as voter policy directives. Perceptions rule the day, but they remain
linked to presidential election outcomes and the president's claim to
be the one voice of the national electorate. Jones (1999) expands the
mandate idea to include a broader view of partisan victory, but retains
the need for a landslide presidential victory. Conley (2001) returns the
study of mandates to a focus on presidential claims, putting Congress
in a reactive mode.

1.2.2 Behavioral Perspectives: What the Voting Tradition *Really* Says about Mandates

Any discussion of election mandates within political science invariably
brings forth a claim that the whole idea of mandates was disproved by

the voting behavior tradition. Mandate claims can't be true, it is said, because we know that voters aren't swayed by issue considerations and can't therefore send messages with their votes. Here we reopen that conclusion by assessing what is actually known from voting research.

Beginning with *The American Voter*, the Michigan school of voting behavior put its emphasis on the relative unimportance of issue considerations as opposed to the claims of party loyalty and the fleeting images of the candidates. But what *The American Voter* did say in this case, and in many others, was far more careful and limited than the exaggerations, almost caricatures, that appeared in the ensuing debates. Campbell, Converse, Miller, and Stokes (1960) were impressed by how little the issue dialogue seemed to matter to ordinary people, probably in contrast to the prevailing nonscientific view, which assumed that voters must be pretty much like the inside the beltway crowd and newspaper op-ed letter writers, who thought of nothing else.

But even this strongest statement stops well short of asserting that issues don't matter, that citizens can't formulate issue positions, can't act on them, or anything of the sort. The emphasis on the lifelong stability of party identification moves in a different direction from treating elections as simple issue referenda, but it does not deny the possibility. "The book," John Kessel (1972) writes,

... sets up three tests for "issue-oriented partisan behavior" – expression of an opinion, perception of what government is doing, and perception of party differences. The book states that between 18 per cent and 36 per cent of the respondents pass these tests, depending upon the issue involved. And of course we now have the benefit of a half century of election experience which tells us that Campbell et al. (1960) were unlucky to have started their enterprize with two quite atypically issue-free contests.

But voting behavior scholarship in the Michigan tradition was just beginning in 1960. *The American Voter* is not the final statement of any of the issues raised in that provocative volume. Over the next fifteen years or so, a lively scholarship emerged. Its agenda was chiefly the claims made by Campbell et al., and its mode was that of the original, exploiting voter surveys for what they could show about the numerous important claims of *The American Voter*.

Under the Michigan tent, flying the banner of quantitative survey research, the community of voting behavior analysts produced a revisionist perspective. As applied to the question of issue voting – the more general question of which the mandate issue is a special case – the revisionist perspective paid homage to Campbell, Converse, Miller, and Stokes (1960), but meanwhile reached a new consensus quite dramatically different than the original. With the benefit of more issue-oriented elections, better survey questions, and the exaggerated *American Voter* claim as perspective, the revisionists found issue voting to be quite widespread and not dependent on high levels of voter sophistication (Alvarez 1997; Carmines and Stimson 1980; Key 1966; Miller and Shanks 1996).

New Micro Understandings. Part of the persuasive case for the unimportance of issue considerations was voters speaking for themselves. When respondents were asked what they liked and disliked about parties and candidates, the language of their replies was sobering. This view of the 1956 electorate in *The American Voter* has an emotional impact on all who read it. Theories of hidden sophistication easily gave way to graphic words, such as the respondent who said, "I don't know much about the man. Our radio's tore up and I ain't heard any news lately" (Campbell et al., 1960, p. 243). More than statistical analyses, such demonstrations seemed to rule out issue understandings of politics. If voters couldn't say why they liked or disliked the parties and candidates, the logical conclusion was that they had no reasons, or at least none more sophisticated than family tradition and candidate images.

What we now know from the better political psychology of recent decades is that failure to be able to reconstruct the facts and arguments that support a conclusion is an expected result. The theory of online processing holds that people listen to facts and arguments, are swayed by them into reaching conclusions that alter their future views but then have little recollection of the basis for those conclusions (Hastie and Park 1986; Lodge, Steenbergen, and Brau 1995). That tells us, importantly, that failure to reconstruct an issue basis for party and candidate evaluations does not mean that issue considerations played no role in forming them. It tells us only that people don't remember much of what they hear, particularly in concerns that are not central to their lives.

Voting and Elections. The phrase "voting and elections" is so common that it is easy to regard the two terms "voting" and "elections" as synonyms. They are not. And that is part of the problem with the generalization of micro voting conclusions about why voters vote as they do to the macro question of what elections mean. When voters are aggregated into an electorate, what is typical of the former does not automatically typify the latter. Thus, even if Campbell et al. had taken the caricatured absolutist position that issues don't matter, even if there had been no revisionists who changed the conclusion to "issues do matter," the conclusion that elections aren't swayed by issue preferences would not have followed.

The meaning of elections is a macro level issue. It emerges in voter movements at the margin. If issue preferences change and elections reflect that change, then issue influence is present even if the modal or typical voter had no such questions in his or her mind. Election outcomes are altered by systematic influence at the margin. In an electorate in which, say, 90 percent of citizens are either blind party loyalists or altogether removed from knowledge of issue controversies, a small number of people behaving systematically can produce all the variation of outcomes that we see between one election and the next. Thus, the only micro voting conclusion that could imply no issue influence in election outcomes is that no citizen ever takes issues into account. Beyond that absolutist and demonstrably false conclusion, the micro voting tradition has nothing to say about the meaning of elections.

What then do we know of macro level issue influence in elections? We know that public mood, a generic set of liberal versus conservative issue positions, is significantly associated with all national election outcomes (Erikson, MacKuen, and Stimson 2002). We know, further, that it is decisively associated with presidential and Senate elections.

It might be said, in sum, that beginning with the idea that the glass of public involvement to in policy debates was full, the authors of *The American Voter* discovered that it was shockingly half empty. Then followed the revisionists, who discovered that it was *only* half empty. Then followed the macro theorists who noted that half was way more than was needed for a meaningful aggregate signal. Interpretation has come full circle, whereas the facts have changed hardly at all.

What then do we really know? We know that mandates exist in the limited sense that election outcomes depend on shifts in public opinion.

Democrats do better when the country is more liberal; Republicans win when it is more conservative. That can't tell us that the more decisive meaning is true, that voters actually intend to send a message. But it surely does not eliminate the possibility.

The study of mandates has advanced our understanding of election results and their impact, but it also has developed in isolation from the normative debate over mandates as threats to democracy. With the exception of Jones's narrowing of the conditions for a true mandate, Dahl's (1990) concerns about the negative repercussions of mandate claims continue to raise a dilemma for democratic governance.

1.3 TELLING THE LARGER STORY OF MANDATE POLITICS

This book is the story of mandate politics. It is a story of significant electoral victories, unexpected victory margins, reassessments of electoral security, and major change in American public policy. The story line touches on much that is important in American politics and political science. Mandates do not flow from every election. We find only the three in the postwar era. They are rare events, but events that explain some of the most important shifts in American public policy. We thus have three stories within the larger story of mandate politics.

The mandate story we present matters because it has governing consequences. Absent the consensual understanding that these elections were properly interpreted to carry a message, America may not have witnessed the dramatic policy and political changes that came about during these three periods. These specific episodes are not politics as usual; rather, they represent unusual politics, politics driven by the mandate dynamic. We know the endings of each of these three stories. The question we address is, how did such change come about? The changes were not inevitable. They may not even have been likely. But they did occur.

We now face the challenge of turning mandate politics into an empirically verified theory that is applicable not just to three particular bills, but applicable across many bills, across entire Congresses, and across elections. In short, we need a scientific version of the story. We lay out the story chronologically, showing how the mandate dynamic forms, influences members of Congress and Congress as a whole, and how it ends. We describe a process that begins with the electorate and works its influence through the social construction of electoral meaning and the strategic calculations of members of Congress. The news of a mandate is important because it carries with it a powerful signal about the relevance of opinion change. To interpret usual signals about opinion change, politicians must ask, "What is the change?" and "Will it actually affect votes?" The mandate message stands apart from the norm because it is decisive, asserting both opinion change and electoral relevance in one capsule.

Chapter 2 begins our analysis with a discussion of how the mandate interpretation is formed. We focus on how unexpected electoral results are socially constructed into a mandate consensus. We look at the preelection expectations, the election results, and the spin attached to them and how it is shaped into a consensual understanding that politics has taken on a new direction. Chapter 3 offers our model of member response. The focus is on the behavioral changes that occur in response to the mandate perception. We document both the initial response and the duration of response of members confronted by news that their electoral world has changed. Our analysis shows that the behavior is real, pervasive, and conditioned by the strength of the mandate perception in the Washington community.

Chapter 3 looks at individual members of Congress, and Chapter 4 investigates the larger pattern of congressional response. It shifts the analysis from the individual member to the aggregate chamber and institution. The analysis documents how the member responses aggregate up to affect the output of an entire Congress. We show how the mandate dynamic is evident to varying degrees in the voting patterns of each chamber and how this shifts the ever important position of the median voter in Congress.

Chapter 5 extends the aggregate analysis one step further by documenting the outcome of the mandates. We show how the mandate affected the passage of major bills and how American public policy shifted as a result. The chapter shows both the immediate impact of the mandate on the political agenda and the shape of public policy as well as the longer term impact on the political system.

We finish our analyses with a look at the aftermath that mandate elections brings. Chapter 6 places our story in the larger context of political dynamics, representation, and policy change. We look at the course of American politics following such dramatic change and the possibility that the thermostatic electorate instigates a corrective if the mandate is perceived as having gone too far. Representational politics is inherently dynamic; public preferences change and political actors shift their behavior in accordance with that change. Mandate politics is a component of this dynamic and to fully understand it, we must look at what reactions it sets in motion. Our analysis is speculative in nature because a full telling of the corrective mechanisms in American politics requires a treatment that would take us too far from the core of our analysis. Our focus is on how mandates arise and how they influence the operation of American politics.

Finally, we conclude in Chapter 7 by moving away from these three times of unusual politics. Instead of focusing on uncovering the effects and implications of these mandate elections, we ask what our theory of mandates tells us about "normal" politics. These years are in many ways distinct from other elections. Studying the unusual in politics provides us leverage over understanding the usual. We think that we have learned a lot about American politics from these three elections. In this last chapter, we put these conclusions into a broader perspective.

2

The Evolution of Mandates

Three Congresses in the modern era have started work in the presence of widespread belief – inside and outside the institution – that their actions would be closely watched by willful voters. The 89th Congress in 1965, the 97th in 1981, and the 104th in 1995 had in common a charged Washington environment, a sense that they must act. This sense, a widely shared belief that they acted under a voter mandate, came from some place and some time before early January, when they began their business. It came, or at least seemed to, from the previous November, from the first Tuesday after the first Monday of that previous November.

But elections do not interpret themselves, do not speak of mandates, do not speak of much of anything except who got how many votes. From somewhere in the campaign, from Election Day, and from the public dialogue after the election, a message arose, was debated, and became agreed on by most people in the Washington community – and by the community of politics outside the beltway. The task of this chapter is find when, how, and from where it came. Our task is to try to understand public dialogues about mandates.

2.1 THE MEDIA SPIN: ON THE DECLARATION OF MANDATES

The idea of electoral mandate may be seen as an objective fact. When voters choose to vote for one party or candidate over another *especially because they wish to send a message about what government should do* and when that message is one-sided, not self-canceling, then an objective electoral mandate exists. Fifty years of voting behavior scholarship, starting with *The American Voter* (Campbell et al. 1960), is skeptical, although not entirely dismissive, that such objective mandates exist at all, that enough voters are sufficiently policy-conscious and free of preexisting party commitments to use their votes to send such messages.

But whatever was or was not in the minds of voters, mandates of a second sort may emerge. These are social constructions, the interpretation and reconstruction of a recent election to support the view that a mandate (of the objective type) did exist. These two senses of the phenomenon are partly independent. Voters could be sending a message that is not received; an objective mandate need not necessarily lead to a socially constructed interpretation of a mandate. And, more likely, the Washington community may receive a message that was never sent. An election that appears to be an otherwise unexplained party sweep may produce a consensus of politicians and commentators that the election carried a message that was not in the mind of voters.

What is crucial about the social construction idea is that it provides the evidence on which government acts. Presidents, members of Congress, lobbyists, and journalistic commentators do not get to look into the minds of individual voters for evidence of objective mandate. What they have before them is a dialogue played out inside the beltway in which some assert that a mandate exists and others agree or disagree. When there is disagreement, then mandate is just partisan spin with no lasting consequence. But when there is consensus, then this consensus itself *is* the socially constructed mandate. In the chapters to come, we shall see that the socially constructed mandate has causal force, changing behaviors and changing policy outcomes. And this is true regardless of whether a mandate of the objective sort ever existed. *Belief* in a mandate has consequences, even if such belief happens to be false.

To observe objective mandates requires both an objective standard of what "counts" as a mandate and analyses of individual level voting behavior that sort out the competing causal forces and observe that sending a policy message was one of the forces. Both have proven nearly impossible to do. There is no objective, defensible standard for how much issue voting is enough to be declared a mandate and the joint simultaneity of virtually all political attitudes makes the challenge of causal sorting more severe than the available data can meet.[1] Although the voting behavior literature continues to have a skeptical stance about electoral mandates, the causal analysis problem is so difficult that the defensible claim is only that we don't know.

Observing socially constructed mandates is altogether an easier thing. We look to the press to stage the dialogue about what elections mean or don't mean. Whether or not there is a consensus in the press is observable from content analysis of postelection interpretive stories. And that is how we proceed.

In order to find out which elections the media portrayed as signaling a shift in popular preferences, we conducted a content analysis of newspaper articles that contain references to an electoral mandate from 1960 through 2002. We look at both presidential elections and off-year elections. A thorough comparison of media coverage across elections is limited by the availability of electronic archives. For the years 1960 through 1978, we analyzed articles from the *New York Times* only. The availability of electronic archives allows us to expand the search from 1980 on to include the *Associated Press*, *United Press International*, and the *Washington Post*. The *New York Times* coverage from 1980 to 2002 is representative of the coverage from the rest of the media sources, so we do not believe that this decision biases our results for the earlier years.

We look to the public expression of interpretations of election outcomes as a means of gauging what members were exposed to in the Washington political environment. Stories about elections vary in frequency of mandate references and in direction. For some years, the issue is rarely discussed. For some it is common fodder. And when the mandate issue is raised, it often is in the context of explicit denial. Some elections provoke journalists to write many stories asserting that the election was *not* a mandate. Thus, we necessarily examine both how often the issue is raised and, when it is, whether the balance of commentary asserts or denies an electoral message.

Figure 2.1 presents a picture of media stories that use the word "mandate" for 1980 through 2002, the period for which we have fully

[1] See Markus and Converse (1979) and Page and Jones (1979) for notable attempts.

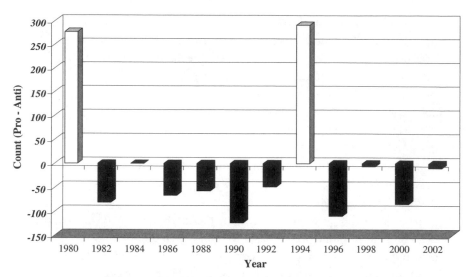

FIGURE 2.1. Balance of Pro- and Antimandate Press Mentions for Election Cycles of 1980–1981 Through 2002–2003. (Source: Compiled by the authors from the *New York Times*, the *Associated Press*, *United Press International*, and *Washington Post*.)

comparable information about the balance of coverage. For each presidential and congressional election we count the number of stories asserting a mandate, from which we subtract the number asserting the contrary. The white bars above the neutral line represent the commentary supportive of mandate interpretations. Years for which the consensus is against mandate interpretations appear in black, below the line. If press coverage captures the Washington insider perspective, and we have no reason to think that it would not, then the story is simple. The elections of 1980 and 1994 are "called" as mandates. Other years in the period are not.

For the years 1960 through 1978, we analyzed articles from the *New York Times* only. Although we have no reason to think that the *Times* is atypical in calling or not calling mandates, our data here (see Table 2.1) are thin and impressionistic. The numbers are so small that single judgment calls loom large in each year. Judgments are necessarily tentative, in no way comparable to the rich media data of the later (electronic) period.

From the primitive data of Table 2.1, 1964 stands out as the only election in which numerous stories assert an electoral mandate and in which those stories are not contradicted by others, claiming the

TABLE 2.1. New York Times *Stories Interpreting Election Outcomes:*
1960 to 1978

Year	Mandate Claim	Total Stories	Percent Supporting Mandate
1960	1	1	100
1962	1	4	25
1964	6	6	100
1966	0	5	0
1968	1	3	33
1970	0	1	0
1972	0	3	0
1974	2	7	29
1976	0	1	0
1978	0	1	0
TOTAL	11	32	34

opposite. As we will see later in the analysis of the numbers election night observers would have seen, 1964 is the single case of stunning impact. The Kennedy win of 1960 draws a single reference to mandate and it is positive. Whether it was the lack of mandate stories or the closest presidential popular vote win[2] in modern history, mandate claims in 1960 were without consequence. The congressional elections of 1966 and 1974 were each rejections of the White House party and not seen as weighty at the time. The 1974 case gave voters their first opportunity to vote against the Watergate scandal and so the one-sided result was far from unexpected.

We tentatively conclude that the elections of 1964, endorsing Lyndon Johnson's "Great Society," 1980, launching the "Reagan revolution," and the midterm election of 1994, the "Contract with America" – becoming a Republican revolution in postelection hyperbola – are the appropriate cases for our investigation of a congressional response.

Why then did these three elections produce a mandate consensus and not others? Is it the elections themselves that drive interpretation? Or is it more subjective, mandates appearing where the winning party effectively works the press to produce them? We turn now to examining the factors that underlie consensus on mandate.

---

[2] Kennedy's winning margin in 1960 was about one-fourth of Al Gore's popular vote "win" of 2000.

2.1.1   Social Construction of Electoral Mandates

"Where do mandates come from?" Answering that question is the task of this chapter. We know at the outset that some time before a new Congress (and usually president) is sworn in a consensus emerges that the previous election carried a message. What we don't know as yet is when and how that consensus emerges.

Mandates are a social construction. Although they often include the belief that their basis is self-evident fact, what they are is an interpretation that comes to be believed because it is asserted often and by diverse sources. We will see in the chapters to come that all cases we have observed are transient, that the interpretation of election results as fundamental new political reality gives way after some time to evidence that nothing fundamental has changed. If mandates were simple facts, and not social construction, this could not be; facts don't change.

Our problem then is to come to terms with the creation of a social construction, to observe the sequence of political dialogues in campaign years and figure out from where the consensus emerges. This is not easily done. For social constructions are a will-o'-the-wisp reality. What we have is a multifaceted public dialogue, in which some people assert an interpretation, others agree, disagree, or ignore it. This is a social process, an emergent reality from the conversation, not the act of any single individual.

We will do our best to understand this process. But the reader should be warned that our best will fall short of the level of confidence we can have when the realities we study are embedded in hard data. We will observe these public conversations and put an interpretation on their character. This topic belongs to that very large class of questions that are inherently interesting, but very hard to answer. But it is a question of central importance to this enterprize and so we are forced to do what we can to come to terms with it.

2.1.2   Spin, Counterspin, and Consensus

After each election, the winning party would like to claim an electoral mandate. The mandate conveys a legitimacy to the party's program that goes beyond winning the White House or gaining seats in Congress. It engages our deepest commitment to democracy, that when the people decide on a course of action, they should prevail. And winning parties regularly do claim a mandate. John Kennedy's 118,000 vote squeaker was declared a mandate by Democratic partisans, as was Jimmy Carter's bigger (but still thin) victory in 1976. Ronald Reagan joined George H. W. Bush's Vice President Dan Quale to call the small 1988 Republican win a mandate from the people. The voters, Bush said, "spoke loud and clear" (*United Press International*, Nov. 9, 1988).

But none can surpass George W. Bush who, having fallen short of his opponent Al Gore by over a half million votes, declared nonetheless that he had a mandate for cutting taxes, changing education, and creating a new energy agenda. "I believe I'm standing here," he said, "because I campaigned on issues that people heard" (*Houston Chronicle*, December 19, 2000).

But consensus requires more. It requires media observers to agree. That is not such a hard thing to do, for the lightly informed commentators often seem to prefer colorful spin to dull fact. But what checks this process is counterspin from the losing party. When winners claim that elections were decisive and voter intentions clear, losers will regularly point to contrary facts and interpretations: the electoral margin was thin, the economy was weak, the candidate was unpopular, the campaign was half-hearted, and so on.

Facts Matter. That's how it goes in normal elections, spin and counterspin producing national disagreement on what, if anything, the election meant. But all is not spin; facts matter. There are rare cases in which the outcome is so decisive, so unexpected, the message so clear, that losers concede rather than counterspin. A *New York Times* account of the Clinton White House following the big Republican gains of 1994 gives the flavor of that one case:

Early this evening, the President and First Lady played host to Democratic donors at a reception in the State Dining Room of the White House, and a senior White House official insisted that their spirit was "not bad." ... But a more candid assessment was offered tonight by one lower-ranking aide to Mr. Clinton as early returns mirrored exit polls in predicting deep Democratic defeats. "It's a blowout," the official said. (*New York Times*, Nov. 8, 1994)

If our simple story of spin and counterspin is an accurate account, then we would predict that the evidence of mandate is likely to be

exaggerated. The winners have a motive to exaggerate and can be expected regularly to do so. The press, longing for a more colorful story
than the usual "The people again demonstrated their indecision over
who should rule and what government should do," will reliably run
with interpretations that exaggerate what the voters intended. Proclaiming dramatic turning points in politics is the bread and butter of
the pundit class. If we take their claims seriously, the nation has turned
so dramatically and so often that our politics should be afflicted with
a fatal case of dizziness. Without a check from the losing party, every
routine election victory can become evidence for unified public sentiment on the course government ought to follow. In a sense, then,
the question "why does mandate consensus occur?" is the same as the
question "why do losing parties sometimes concede?"

2.2   BEFORE THE ELECTION

Spin doesn't begin on election night. The campaigns from beginning
to end are more interpretation than fact. Candidates and parties uniformly claim that their messages are drawing public response. We
would be surprised by candor in such matters.

But the skepticism of party competition undermines all these claims.
When everybody lies, nobody believes. It is part of the lore of American
politics that the public deeply discounts everything it hears in campaign
season. People understand that political campaigns and carnival mid-
ways are places where it is foolish to expect the simple truth.

The press is the same. It treats campaigns as occasions for sport
lying, assuming that nothing either side says is to be taken as more
than strategic construction of reality. And more, the subject of much
complaint, journalistic coverage of campaigns rarely gives emphasis to
issues. To read the coverage of campaigns later taken to have produced
mandates is to see the same old thing, who's ahead and who's behind
dominating coverage in lieu of treatment of issues or response to them.
The flavor of these historic occasions is not discernably different from
that of campaigns in which we later decide that voters did not speak.

The 1980 campaign is an apt example. In that year, later proclaimed
the "Reagan revolution," one would not have seen it coming from
reading press accounts. In January and February, while Reagan was
proposing his giant supply side tax cut program, press attention focused

on whether or not Reagan's "Rose Garden" strategy would be effective in the early primaries.[3] (It wasn't.) And then in New Hampshire in March the big story was the brouhaha over control of the microphone at the Republican debate. How voters were responding to the massive tax cut and implied major diminution of the scope of the U.S. federal government we did not learn.

The consequence of all this skepticism is that nothing before election results come in seems to register. It is as if we have the collective attitude, "We'll see" in response to all claims. Why this is the case is not obvious. We do have preelection polls. And inferring voter response to message is not more difficult from voting intention than it is from actual votes.

2.3 ELECTION NIGHT

Those who comment on American political life learn two things as the votes are counted on election night: whether or not the win is large and whether or not it comes as expected. Both matter for the social construction of mandate. The size of the win is necessary for the claim that it is a party sweep. And when the sweep is unexpected, commentators are forced to invent a story line that can account for it. We deal separately with the two.

2.3.1 Size of the Win

Election night presents commentators and the public evidence both of particular elections and of patterns across election types. We learn most about the presidency, if it is a presidential year, less (pretty much in this order) about U.S. Senate seats, gubernatorial elections, and seats in the U.S. House. No matter how big the win at the top of the ticket, contradictory patterns lower down undermine the conclusion that the winning party is sweeping the night.

Thus, it is important to assess both how well the parties do in particular contests and how uniform their showing is. When the victory is both big and uniform, then commentators have something important

---

[3] Not yet president and not using it for effect, Reagan's handlers knew that their elderly candidate tired easily and that his performances were badly affected by fatigue. They sought to keep him fresh by running a long-distance media campaign and keeping the candidate rested for the later fray. The strategy was shelved after a terrible showing in the Iowa caucuses.

TABLE 2.2. *Measures of the Election Outcome*

Concept	Indicator	Mean	Standard Deviation
Presidency	Percent Democratic of Two-Party Vote (Standardized)	0.0	1.0
Senate	Democratic Seat Gains or Losses (Standardized)	0.0	1.0
House	Democratic Seat Gains or Losses (Standardized)	0.0	1.0
Governors	Democratic Gains or Losses (Standardized)	0.0	1.0

to explain and voters sending a message is likely to emerge as an explanation.

To capture these phenomena – and to emulate what commentators would have seen as election results poured in – we display comparable indicators for four offices. The comparability is achieved by standardizing over the historical data of 1960–2002. The standardization allows graphic presentation of the multiple offices together. And it yields a natural interpretation. Values near zero signal tight contests. Positive numbers show a Democratic advantage, negative similarly a Republican one. The four indicators are displayed in Table 2.2.

Outcomes for the elections of 1960 through 1980 are displayed in Figure 2.2. For each election year, the net result for four offices is shown if it is a presidential year, three if not. For the set of offices, we ask whether the wins are large or small and whether they are consistent across the multiple office contexts. Observe 1960, for example. The presidential race was an historically close contest and the trivial edge to the Democrats is more than offset by losses in Senate and House contests. Clearly, there is no party surge, no need to invent an explanation for one. The 1962 contest is again a split verdict, with Senate Democratic gains offset by House losses.

The races in the early 1960s set up a contrast with 1964. There we have the best Democratic showing in the presidency of this electoral era coupled with a very strong showing in the House, a small Democratic gain in the Senate,[4] and the one contradiction, the loss of one

---

[4] And this is more impressive than it looks. The Democrats gained seats on top of the best class (1958) of modern times. With all of those 1958 seats at risk, the Democrats would have been expected to lose some ground in a normal election.

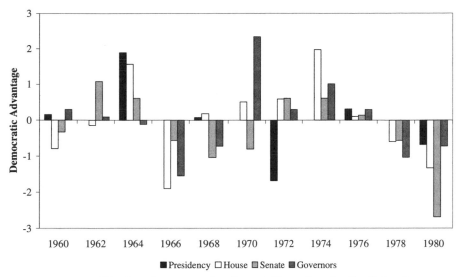

FIGURE 2.2. Election Outcomes for Four Offices (Standardized) by Year: 1960–1980.

governorship. These are the kind of results that both impress and demand explanation.

Based only on election results, 1966, with all three contests moving toward the GOP, could have produced a mandate claim. It did not. The election result was essentially a give-back of the 1964 Democratic wins, except of course that Lyndon Johnson remained in the White House. And Republican gains in House and Senate merely reduced the size of very large Democratic majorities in both bodies.

The contests of 1968, 1970, and 1972 are all mixed verdicts. Of these, 1972 is most notable. It combines a Republican landslide at the presidential level, a usual spur to mandate talk, with Democratic wins in all other kinds of races. The heavy Democratic majorities that would investigate the Watergate scandal and ultimately chase Richard Nixon from office were created in part from Nixon's failure to do anything for his party while he was creating an impressive showing for himself.

The Watergate scandal was the story line of 1974, when Democrats prevailed everywhere. As a midterm election and one with a ready explanation for party success, the impressive wins created no interpretive stir. Jimmy Carter's narrow win in 1976 was matched by near tie elections for other offices, a normal election. It was followed by the

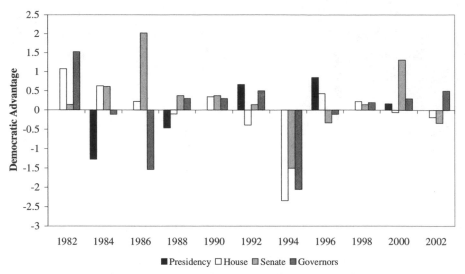

FIGURE 2.3. Election Outcomes for Four Offices (Standardized) by Year: 1982–2002.

predictable midterm loss in 1978, but the size and scope of Republican gains that year might have foretold a bit of the electoral future.

Election night 1980 needed a story. Republicans shocked the nation and the commentators (more on surprise is to come) with a *big* presidential win, when, against an incumbent, even a small one would have impressed. But 1980 also produced an impressive GOP gain in the House, the party's biggest ever win in the Senate (producing a then-unheard-of Republican majority in that body), and gains in statehouses.

A sour economy helped Democrats regain some of that lost ground in 1982 (see Figure 2.3 for the elections of 1982 through 2002). This was followed by another Republican landslide in 1984, much like Nixon's twelve years before, which produced Democratic gains in Congress. These big presidential wins generate a lot of spin about voters speaking their mind. But the spin fails to become more than spin when it cannot explain how the opposite message seems to have motivated voting for other offices.

The four elections of 1986 through 1992 produced either mixed party results or, in the case of 1990, uniform Democratic wins but too small to matter. But there is no mistaking the 1994 outcome.

Republicans won at all levels and won big, regaining control of the Senate and taking control of the House for the first time in forty years. This outcome, contested against the background of solid growth in the economy, demanded an explanation for why voters turned out so many of the president's partisans.

The elections of 1996 through 2002, like the set of four between 1986 and 1994, produced no party sweeps except for 1998, when the Democratic gains were uniform but also very small. The most recent one, 2002, provides a snapshot of the disconnect between spin and mandate. This election produced two weeks of talk of extraordinary gains and "historic" turns built on an outcome best described as "ho-hum." The spin in these cases doesn't take. After a few days of media buzz, it just goes away.

In sum, there appear to be three types of elections. In most years, the outcomes are divided, where neither party decisively wins across the board. In a few cases (maybe 1966, 1974, 1978, and 1982) we have one-sided outcomes, but elections that have a readily available nonmandate explanation. Finally, we have three cases where there are sizable gains for one party across all types of elections without an easy counterexplanation. These are the years that get declared mandates.

We've used two figures to display quite a lot of data about election returns. The motivation for all these numbers is not to have to assume what is important, to try to get the feel of election night as the numbers are reported. Now, for a summary look, we just add them all up, producing one measure of party surges across all four offices (equally weighted).[5]

Figure 2.4 provides that summary look. The 1994 midterm election emerges as the most one-sided in party terms, followed by 1980 and 1964. These (we have seen) are the three cases that produced a consensus interpretation of electoral mandate in the early postelection period. The midterms of 1966 and 1974 are almost as large in total effect as 1964, but then did not need a mandate interpretation. The 1966 result mainly simply reversed the Democratic gains of 1964. And 1974, the Watergate election, was long expected to be a Democratic sweep.

---

[5] The commentators of course do not equally weight. The presidency gets the lion's share of election coverage. Well known names in Senate races come next. And the House and gubernatorial races are just barely mentioned.

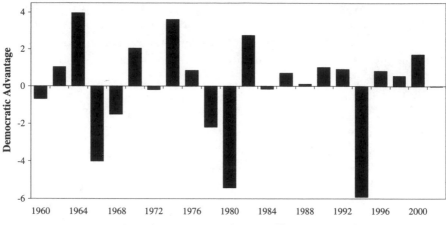

FIGURE 2.4. Cumulative Impact of Four Office Outcomes by Year.

And neither of these midterm elections affected majority control of Congress.

2.3.2 Blindsiding

The size of the party win matters, but it isn't everything. We postulate that *unexpected* Election Day results more readily call for mandate explanations. When, for example, popular incumbent presidents are reelected by big margins, we see it coming many months in advance. We expect presidents to be reelected and don't look for explanations when they are. It is election night blindsiding, the result that nobody saw coming, that demands attention.

When an election result is expected, commentators sort it out and explain what is coming weeks in advance of Election Day. Their stock-in-trade, the economy is good or bad, the president is popular or unpopular and so forth, explains the result that is going to happen. Then when it does happen, there is no further need for explanation. On election night when the result is *not* what was expected, it is quite different. Then commentators are grasping for a handle, trying to explain a pattern in the result that nobody had expected. Then they are particularly likely to bring out the simple idea that the voters were sending a message.

Ronald Reagan's forty-nine-state electoral college victory in 1984 serves as an example of how expectations can deprive a big win of meaning. In addition to the losses in Congress that muddied the

Republican triumph, there was never much doubt that Reagan would be reelected. After the economic recovery of 1983–1984, the "Gipper" was in good favor with the electorate. His campaign slogan, "It's morning in America," captured the good feeling of which he was chief beneficiary. It was reflected in the polls, where leads of twenty points or more over Mondale were routine throughout the campaign, including on election eve. The median of six election eve polls had Reagan with 59.2 percent of the two-party split. His huge win was 59.0 percent. On election night there was nothing to explain.

The import of the unexpected puts congressional and presidential races in somewhat different light. The presidency is the central focus of American politics. But because the presidency is so important, presidential races are very well predicted. We routinely report hundreds of "horse race" polls, with as many as five or six per day in the final days. And the state-by-state outcomes are predicted from state polls, which are even more numerous. The consequence of all this activity and expense is that our election eve expectations for the presidential race are very well informed. The median of the election eve polls misses the mark by about a percent or so on average (see Table 4.1 in Stimson, 2004). In most presidential elections, the only way to be surprised on Election Day is not to pay attention.

We do not do anything like that in the case of congressional elections. Calling the House outcomes in particular is plagued by the mismatch of national survey organizations to the 435 individual races. Because sampling designs rarely fit congressional districts, national surveys rely on some variation of what has come to be called the "generic" House voting question. The Gallup organization asks:

If the elections for Congress were being held today, which party's candidate would you vote for in your Congressional district, the Democratic party's candidate or the Republican party's candidate?

The generic question has two problems that greatly impede its forecasting accuracy. One is that it is generic, that the contest between and a "Democrat" and a "Republican" will not always elicit the same response as the actual ballot, on which one of the named candidates is likely to be well known and popular, the other not. The second problem is that most of the respondents in these surveys live in districts where the outcome is one-sided and pretty much predetermined. Some even reside where there is no legal contest, where only one party fields a candidate. On average, about 5 to 10 percent of the 435 districts are considered "in play" by those who closely follow the congressional contests. Survey respondents from these districts are giving useful information in response to the generic question. The problem is numbers. Five to ten percent of a typical survey of 1,000 is 50 to 100 people! That just isn't enough to produce statistically reliable estimates. (And our limited concern with the congressional races doesn't justify the huge expense of surveying massive samples, say 10,000 or so, to get the needed numbers from contested districts.) In consequence, we do not do very well forecasting the congressional outcome. In a lopsided race, the generic polls will generally get the direction right. But that is about as much as can be said, and there is no guarantee even of that.

The consequence of this digression into polling is that elections for the House of Representatives have a considerable opportunity to surprise on Election Day. Presidential races generate mandate interpretations when their outcome is unexpected. But that is rarely the case. Big wins in the House are *always* unexpected; our expectations just aren't that good.

The evidence of congressional elections is also often cleaner than that of the presidency. There are always many explanations for winning or losing the presidency. Many of these are personal and idiosyncratic. Candidates do well or badly because they are popular or not, because they campaign well or badly, because they have a good or bad record to run on. These things always matter. And they are intermixed with the voters' intentions. And so a win is easy to explain.

The Clinton versus Dole contest of 1996 is illustrative. Clinton was personally popular. As all sitting presidents, he was more "presidential" than his opponent. His record of success in managing the economy was enviable. Dole "never got traction" it was said. He tried one theme after another and got no enthusiastic response to any. He tried to tell prosperous Americans that things weren't as good as they seemed, a hard sell. Thus, as Clinton coasted to an easy victory, there was no need ask whether voters were sending a message about the Clinton-Dole divide over the size of government. There were plenty of reasons to expect a Clinton win without recourse to messages.

Congressional, and particularly House, elections present more systematic evidence of party fortunes. If one party is winning all the contested races, one doesn't assume that it has the advantage in the personal and idiosyncratic in every district. More likely, something national is moving all together. And a leading candidate for explaining a national surge is always that voters are speaking their minds.

The conclusion of this logic, somewhat surprising we think, is that mandates will often be made more from congressional than from presidential elections. The presidency, the contest that draws all our interest and attention, is not by itself likely to produce a mandate interpretation. The more systematic evidence of surges in congressional, gubernatorial – sometimes even state legislative – races comes to the fore for such claims.

2.3.3 Three Election Nights

Here we take a more particularistic look at our three mandate cases, tracing the election year horse race polls and looking at the expectations for the race before the votes began to come in. It seems to be a feature of American political life that we tend to reconstruct our memories of these decisive cases, believing that we saw them coming. Reading what was written and what potential voters declared before anyone could know the outcome is a useful corrective.

1964. The 1964 election campaign was framed by Lyndon Johnson's personal popularity in the wake of the Kennedy assassination and by fratricide in the Republican Party's effort to pick an opponent. The Republican contest was bitter in the beginning and got worse leading into a nominating convention that produced Barry Goldwater and doomed his chances of running a successful contest. An incumbent president, only one year in office, benefitting from a surge of public support in response to the assassination, and with a booming economy, was not likely to lose. But with the considerable assistance of Goldwater himself, given to colorful but ill-considered statements, Goldwater's opponents for the Republican nomination had pictured him as a wild man, capable of starting a nuclear war, ending social security, and generally a threat to the public order.[6] So battered was he by opposition within his own camp that there was little left for Johnson to do.

[6] See White (1965) for a colorful account of the GOP primary and nomination war.

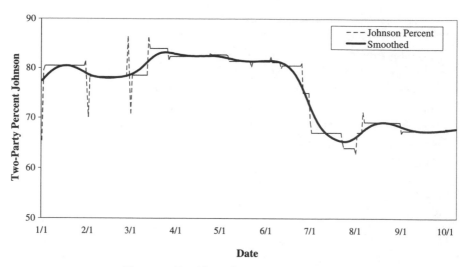

FIGURE 2.5. The 1964 Presidential Horse Race: Johnson Percentage.

To gauge Election Day expectations for the 1964 outcome we assemble all the available "horse race" polls pitting Lyndon Johnson against opponent Barry Goldwater. From these, we solve for a daily time-series of the Johnson percentage of the two candidate vote intentions using the dimensional extraction system of Stimson (1991, 1998). To further summarize these data we solve for a smooth representation of the polling data, that is, one without day-to-day fluctuation due to sampling error, using the Hodrick-Prescott filter.

These data are seen in Figure 2.5, which captures the extraordinary Johnson lead throughout the election year. Our interpretation is that the unprecedented lead early in the year, roughly until the campaign began with the party conventions, is a carry-over of the nation's emotional response to the Kennedy assassination of November 1963. Johnson quickly grabbed the mantle of JFK's successor and the nation converted shock and grief into political support. As the campaign gained focus in late summer Johnson's numbers dropped from unprecedented to merely "landslide" proportions. It was not a suspenseful election night. The polls predicted a blowout presidential election and that is what occurred.

But election night 1964 was not without its surprises. Although all the attention was focused on the presidency, Democrats added to their already huge Senate majority and, picking up thirty-seven seats, scored one of the biggest wins of all time in House elections. The result, which we have seen neither before or since, was a White House that could produce legislation at will, using a supermajority so large – 295 Democrats to 140 Republicans – that Republicans had no role at all and moderate Democrats were steamrolled by a liberal majority.

Election night 1964 confirmed the expected Johnson win. His 61 percent of the popular vote, the largest since Franklin Roosevelt's 1936 win, gave him the landslide for which he had hoped. He had asked for a mandate, "loud and clear." Early in the evening, as one after another, traditionally Republican leaning states fell into the Johnson column, it became both loud and clear. Stunned observers watched as the Republicans failed even in their bastions, all of New England, all of the Midwest, and then all of the West – except Barry Goldwater's home in Arizona (itself a close call). In an era of slower moving media technology it would be Thursday morning before the full extent of the Democratic win became apparent. Tom Wicker, on the front page of *New York Times*, said of it:

The Republican party, divided by Barry Goldwater and smashed by Lyndon B. Jonson, surveyed yesterday the wreckage of one of the worst election defeats in American History.

From the Pacific Coast through the so-called Republican heartland in the Middle West to the New England hills, the Democratic party stood triumphant – and by some of the most remarkable margins ever recorded. (*New York Times*, Nov. 5, 1964, p. 1)

After the very close election of 1960, the three television networks invested heavily in computing technology in order to be able to call the winner earlier and more accurately than their competitors. For the presidential election of 1964, the investment was wasted, for one could have known from early returns, even several hours before most polls closed, that a sweep was underway.[7] The only suspense was whether it would prove to be the most decisive ever. It did.

Although Goldwater was losing as expected, the toll on other Republicans was more surprising. Two household names, Kenneth Keating of New York and Robert A. Taft Jr. of Ohio, lost key Senate

---

[7] The earliest indicators were rural Kansas, Kentucky, and Indiana, all heavily Republican, all going for Johnson.

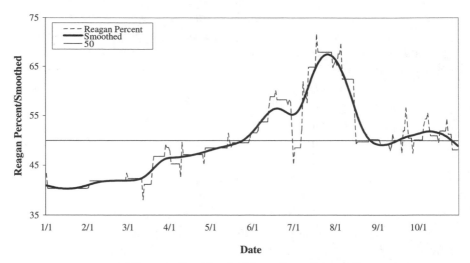

FIGURE 2.6. The 1980 Presidential Horse Race: Reagan Percentage.

races, whereas a third, Hugh Scott of Pennsylvania, barely survived a challenge from a largely unknown opponent. In the House, the numbers told the story. It was simply a Democratic sweep.

1980. Jimmy Carter was a wounded president in the 1980 campaign. Exceedingly popular a year before it mattered, Carter in 1980 suffered a recession in the domestic economy combined with a yearlong inability to deal with a hostage crisis in Iran. His weakness drew a challenge from Teddy Kennedy for the Democratic nomination. Ultimately unsuccessful, Kennedy managed to best the president in several primaries. At the end, Kennedy had the momentum, whereas Carter had the delegates necessary for nomination. Carter was vulnerable.

On Election Day 1980, nonetheless, a careful student of the polls (see Figure 2.6) would have concluded that the presidential election would be very close and that Ronald Reagan appeared to be fading. Both conclusions were quite wrong. The outcome was not close at all and it was Reagan, not Jimmy Carter who had the last minute momentum. Election night was a *big* surprise.[8]

---

[8] Although one who was not surprised was Jimmy Carter, whose private polling by Pat Cadell showed the last minute Reagan momentum and Reagan's quickly widening lead. Carter was primed to concede before the results were in.

The story of the 1980 campaign in Figure 2.6 is one of early Carter dominance. As the campaign year began, Carter's standing was high and the Republicans appeared to be obliging him by nominating Ronald Reagan, the candidate the Carter people thought easiest to beat. In the background, not part of the campaign, but on the evening news every night, was the holding of fifty-two American diplomatic hostages in Iran. The hostage incident, initially a source of support for Carter, was dragging on without resolution and dragging down Carter as time passed and he was unable to do anything about the embarrassment. A rescue attempt in April was aborted when helicopters were lost in a desert sandstorm on the way to Tehran, with eight of the rescuers killed in a collision after the mission was aborted. That failure, for which Carter took personal responsibility, punctuated the growing disaffection over his inability to act. Combined with a midyear recession in the American economy, Carter's reelection prospects were increasingly troubled.

By midyear, as Carter was surviving the Kennedy challenge, suffering failures in the economy simultaneous with his inability to do anything about the hostage crisis, the Reagan challenge began to look formidable. As so often is the case, the initial surge of support for a president in crisis – the failed rescue mission – was replaced by disillusionment when the crisis could not be resolved.

Closely watching the polls, the press was prepared for a nail-biter. *Newsweek*'s headline story, a week before Election Day 1980, was "A Poll Shows Carter Moving Up":

Jimmy Carter and Ronald Reagan are running dead even as they come to the final week of Campaign '80 – but according to the latest *NEWSWEEK* Poll, shifts in voter perceptions, especially on issues relating to war and peace, suggest that the President has somewhat greater potential to win a decisive edge by Election Day. These trends could be altered by any dramatic developments in this week's debate or in the maneuvering over the U.S. hostages in Iran, but they nonetheless constitute a clear pattern of progress for Carter since his dog days this summer. (*Newsweek*, Nov. 3, 1980)

The final preelection edition one week later reported a virtual dead heat, Carter forty-three and Reagan forty-four, in line with Las Vegas odds that had Reagan odds at six to five in the week before the election. The actual Reagan win by about ten points – accompanied by major gains in House, Senate, and gubernatorial elections – then became "a landslide of stunning dimension" (*Newsweek*, Nov. 17, 1980).

These two weeks bracket an expectation swinging from a likely indication of a Carter win to a result that was shocking in contrast to expectation. With the polls showing an election too close to call, preelection observers naturally disagreed in calling the winner. But nobody forecast a Reagan landslide. A cautious analyst, looking at the polls, would have been sure that the race would be close, unsure who would come out on top. When the race was not close an explanation for the jarring result was needed. The explanation was mandate.

No other elections can crowd out the presidential contest from the center of public attention. But the shocking reverses of Democratic Senate candidates came close on election night 1980. It was a rout. Going down to defeat were some of the best known and most popular senators of the era, George McGovern of South Dakota, John Culver of Iowa, Birch Bayh of Indiana, and Warren Magnuson of Washington. In the House John Brademas, a key Democratic leader, was defeated. Howard Baker Jr., who would become the Republican majority leader in the new Senate, called it "... the biggest, most historic political event of this century," and, shortly after the polls closed, said, "I smell a landslide" (*New York Times*, Nov. 5, 1980).

1994. The proposal, debate, and eventual failure of the Clinton national health insurance proposal was the lead-in to the congressional elections of 1994. Republicans faced the elections with an enthusiasm not seen before. After winning the health care battle, it seemed possible that they also might win the House election, a feat they had not achieved in forty years.

In presidential races the horse race polls are front page and prime time material. Most voters probably have a good sense of how the race is going. In midterm congressional elections, in contrast, the generic congressional polls are chiefly an insider's game. So when we look at the development of the 1994 contest through the polls, it is useful to remember that not many Americans knew what they showed. The presidential horse race polls can to some degree reconstruct how the election felt day by day. The greater reality of congressional contests is that they do not "feel" at all. Before the last days of the preelection period, most voters are scarcely aware that a contest is underway

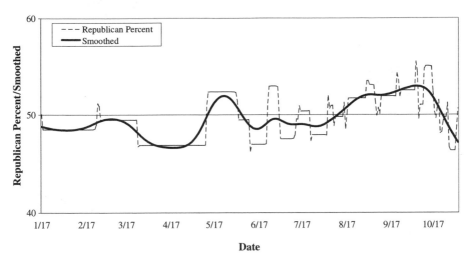

FIGURE 2.7. The 1994 Congressional Horse Race: Republican Percentage.

and – we don't know this for sure – probably do not have very accurate expectations of the outcome.

If we had been watching the development of the 1994 contest, we would have seen that the numbers were useful in historical context. The usual congressional election question was how big the Democratic majority would be, how many more Americans were reporting that they would vote for the local Democratic candidate. For much of the summer and fall of 1994 Figure 2.7 shows a majority reporting Republican support. Never very large, and contradicted by a Democratic surge near Election Day, taken seriously the polls highlighted the possibility of an unusual election.

Election night 1994 was a shocker. The suggestion from the final days that congressional elections would produce the Democratic majority did not predict the outcome at all. That outcome, as we have seen, was big and wholly one-sided. And the drama was more than numbers. Mario Cuomo, often the leading figure in Democratic presidential speculation, could not hold the governorship of New York. And, most visible of all, Thomas Foley, Speaker of the House, did not have to face the indignity of becoming mere minority leader; he lost his seat outright to an unknown Republican challenger.

Although it was clear that result was a Republican sweep of historic proportion, on election night control of the House was not yet determined. And, indeed, much of the story of what 1994 meant was not yet told on election night.

To write of election night is for most of us to think of being positioned before the living room television set watching the drama unfold. Television itself becomes part of the mandate story.

2.3.4   The Filter of TV Commentary

It matters that Americans get their election news – and the views that are packaged with it – overwhelmingly from television. Print is too slow for fast breaking news and radio is a news medium largely for people on the go, which not many are on Tuesday evenings after 8:00 P.M. Eastern. Unlike nearly all other news, from which newspapers, magazines, and radio use their peculiar strengths to compete for a part of the public's attention, election night is virtually all television.

The consequence of this fact is that the characteristics of the medium, and its "personalities," infuse the story of the election outcome. The most striking of these is that TV is a complexity filter; simple ideas and analyses pass through the filter and into public consciousness, complex ones do not. Because political reality is complex, distortion is inevitable. The competition between simple and complex or subtle interpretations is a fixed game; simple wins every time.

By the usual estimates the policies and people who determine what goes out on the airwaves pitch the content to about a ninth grade level of understanding. Stories that require more sophisticated understanding tend not to get told at all. But TV has to cover elections. So if one accepts the idea that understanding political reality requires more than ninth grade background, then accurate election interpretation just can't be done. This is consistent with the stylized fact of voting behavior analysts, that election night interpretation of patterns is almost always wrong.

The "who" of television commentary is part of the story. The election night lineup includes three sorts of people. The anchor people and those who report from remote sites think of themselves as journalists and are bound by the constraint of journalistic standards of fact and interpretation, or at least by a more limited standard appropriate for narrating a story as it develops in real time. Pundits are called on to make sense of the fact pattern. Most often they are from the editorial end of the business, where being fast, colorful, certain, and simple are more valued than being right. Not much constrained by fact at all, the pundits are often busy "finding" facts that fit a story predetermined by their partisan and ideological commitments. The stories they tell are very much determined by which of them get air time.[9] Last are the technical analysts, often experts in survey research. Their role, like the ceremonial appearance of accountants at the Academy Awards, is to give a patina of respectability – in this case, science – to the night's storytelling; they are not part of the real show.

Could TV tell a thoughtful story on election night? The data are a severe constraint. What is known as exit polls and state-by-state results flow in is at best painfully superficial. The results raise questions, but they aren't at all good for answering them. Time, in contrast, is probably not a constraint. As all election night viewers know, a very large proportion of election coverage is time filling, saying something in the long spaces between bursts of hard news. So there is plenty of air time for analysis. The greater limitation is TV's self-imposed viewer IQ limit.

So we expect television analysis regularly to be wrong in the direction of being too simple. And, of course, the mandate idea is as simple as it gets. Why is party A doing so well? Because the voters endorsed party A's program. That's all it takes. Of course, it also takes a willingness to claim unknowns facts, what the voters were thinking, but the pundits are seldom slowed by needed facts; they can be created.

Other explanations are more complex, multivariate, and less concise. A reckoning of 1980, for example, would have to take account of an election year recession, of Jimmy Carter's impaired standing due to the yearlong hostage crisis, of candidate personal appeals, and then *also* of voters sending a message.

Always there are alternative explanations for a party win. Real politics is complex, real explanations multivariate. So it is a considerable challenge to settle on "voters sending a message." In 1964, for example, the opponent Barry Goldwater was widely viewed as a radical, out

---

[9] Alterman (2003) argues that TV pundits rise to the top of their profession from the ability to speak to complex issues in simple "sound bite" analyses, often while barren of any knowledge of the subject. This is a selection process that seems not to favor thoughtful people.

of the mainstream, even within his own party. He talked somewhat casually about using nuclear weapons at a time when fear of nuclear war was quite gripping. And Lyndon Johnson had the wind of prosperity in his sails. Some voters were proclaiming devotion to the fallen John F. Kennedy by voting for his successor. And these things were real, not just party rhetoric for rationalizing a loss.

In 1994, it was argued that Democrats simply didn't turn out in normal numbers. This explanation is probably quite short of the mark of explaining the sweeping Republican victory. And turnout is not accurately known until well after Election Day. To understand how the idea of mandate developed in 1994 – and in other years – we need to examine how the election interpretation evolves in the weeks and months after the counting is over.

2.4   THE BUILDUP TO TAKING OFFICE

We wish to understand the public dialogue over election interpretation after the fact. To do so we perform a content analysis of major print media sources[10] for our three mandate election cases. Unlike earlier analyses (that focused on the question, mandate or not?), here we wish to get a feeling for the more complex dialogue. Our data are from press stories mentioning "election" and "president," "Congress," or "governor," spanning the period from morning after Election Day to the swearing in of the new Congress in early January. We code explanations, any attempt to account for the result, ignoring other materials. We look mainly at paragraphs in news stories and editorials, secondarily at headlines.

Explaining the Election Outcome. Journalists, politicians, and scholars explain election outcomes after the fact. And the first two of these

[10] The sources vary by year from changes in electronic availability. Our most complete set, for 1994, includes the *New York Times* and *Washington Post*, a set of important regional papers, *Atlanta Journal Constitution, Boston Globe, Denver Post, Houston Chronicle, Minneapolis Star Tribune, Seattle Times*, and *San Francisco Chronicle* plus two newsweeklies, *Newsweek* and *US News and World Report*. For 1980, we have the four national sources, the *Post, Times*, and the two newsweeklies. For 1964, we have only the *Times*. Because of this noncomparability, we were prepared to analyze these data separately by election. We have seen, however, that the news sources are highly similar and so we merge the data for most analyses.

TABLE 2.3. *A Summary of Election Explanations*

Election Explanation	Percent
Voter Mandate	51.9
Issues and Ideology	18.8
Issues, Republicans Too Conservative (1964)	0.8
Issues, Contract with America (1994)	0.5
Campaign Tactics	8.8
Candidate Attractiveness	6.0
Performance, Peace and Prosperity	2.9
Mandate Denial	2.6
Other Explanations	7.7
TOTAL	100.0

do so in public in the immediate aftermath. Elections being a complex interweave of candidate, strategies, and voter preferences, there are a lot of ways one can account for the same facts. The simplest is to say that the voters spoke, that they knew what the parties and candidates were offering and chose what they preferred. This is the mandate explanation. For our three elections that generated a consensus on mandate, it is the dominant explanation, appearing in 52 percent of all election explanations (see Table 2.3).[11]

Almost indistinguishable is an emphasis on issues and ideology. Saying that 1964 voters rejected Barry Goldwater's conservative views is not quite the same as saying they supported his opponent Lyndon Johnson. But the one leads naturally to the other. About 19 percent of all election commentary stresses issues and ideology. And there are two special cases of issue commentary. In 1964, the postelection press was filled with commentary that the Republicans needed to reorganize their party, in effect to dump the Goldwater conservatives in control of the apparatus, to have any chance in future elections (1 percent). And in 1994 one could point to support for the "Contract with America" as a specific election explanation (about 0.5 percent). Together, mandate claims and the various issue explanations account for 71 percent of all election explanations in these years. We combine these in analyses to come.

---

[11] Our unit of analysis for coding the election explanations is the paragraph. Election stories may have several and they are rarely all the same. Headlines, coded separately, are not included in this analysis.

The staple explanations of normal election outcomes form the alternative to mandate and issue accounts. Candidates may win or lose because they chose good or (more often) bad tactics on which to fight the campaign. The preferred explanation of losers, tactical references account for about 9 percent of all election explanations. "We weren't unified. We didn't get our people out to vote. We campaigned in the wrong places." This one hears a lot from the losing side. If there is a standard press story of American elections, it is that attractive candidates running good campaigns beat unattractive candidates running uninspired campaigns. What is notable in Table 2.3 is that these old standards account for only 6 percent of all election explanations. Candidate attractiveness clearly does matter in American elections, but gets pushed to the side as an explanation when the hotter copy of voter intent is available for explanation. So, too, is performance in office. A dominant explanation for party wins and losses in political science, matters of peace and prosperity don't figure importantly (3 percent) in explaining mandate elections. Political scientists would explain much of the 1964 and 1980 outcomes as due to Lyndon Johnson's prosperity and Jimmy Carter's recession.[12]

Two other categories round out the possibilities. One is stories that explicitly deny mandate and issue explanations. Often sourced to the losing party, these are challenges to the dominant interpretation. In the face of overwhelming consensus that the 1964 verdict reflected rejection of Goldwater's conservative views, for example, F. Clifton White, Goldwater's campaign manager, said, "...conservatism wasn't defeated in this election; it was hardly even debated" (*New York Times*, Nov. 23, 1964). Pat Caddell, Jimmy Carter's 1980 pollster, took the same tack, disputing the notion that the

heavy losses suffered by liberal Senators and Representatives represented a major party realignment in the country. All those who lost tonight were in trouble of their own in recent days.... There is nothing in the data I've seen so far to suggest a major ideological shift in the country from liberal to conservative views. (*New York Times*, Nov. 5, 1980)

---

[12] Barry Goldwater agreed on the 1964 verdict, asserting *after* the election that no Republican (except perhaps Dwight Eisenhower) could have overcome the Johnson prosperity record in 1964. Although the statement served to direct attention away from his own candidacy and (particularly) his conservative platform, it is in line with subsequent political science scholarship.

TABLE 2.4. *Mandate Explanations by Year, Percent*

Summary Mandate Position	Election Year			Total
	1964	1980	1994	
Mandate and Issue Explanations	82	68	69	71
Other Explanations	18	32	31	29
TOTAL	100	100	100	100

Other sorts of explanations, for example reference to the Iran hostage crisis in 1980, account for the remaining 8 percent.

In Table 2.4, we break out all election explanations into two types, those basically supporting mandate claims (mandates, general issues, and specific issues in Table 2.3) and all others and examine them by election year. The basic message we see in the table is that the three elections are much alike. The greater focus on mandate in 1964 is probably due to the postelection struggle for control of the Republican Party, which featured numerous claims from Republican moderates that Goldwater's conservative views had caused the sweeping election defeat.

Explanation Winnowing. Marjorie Hershey's (1992) analysis of the 1984 campaign postelection period, a model for our own analysis, points to "winnowing" as the dominant feature of the journalistic landscape after election day.[13] Her analysis shows a pattern of numerous competing explanations for the election in the immediate aftermath that eventually gets winnowed down to a smaller set of standard explanations over time. This winnowed set becomes the popular wisdom, the "everybody knows" explanations of future reference to the contest.

We find no such pattern in our three elections. This is not, we think, a matter of perspective or of method but, rather, reflects a genuine difference between a hard election (combining a GOP presidential landslide with Republican losses in both houses of Congress) such as 1984 and the easier cases of mandates. In our cases, the mandate interpretation emerges immediately and dominates throughout. There is no winnowing because the story is basically simple from the outset.

[13] See also Thomas and Baas (1996) for analysis of 1992.

The Press: A Singular Voice. One might think that the press would interpret election outcomes at least in part from its leanings. We see no evidence that it does. An analysis of how the election is explained produces no interesting variation – very little variation at all – across media outlets. The *New York Times* and *Washington Post*, for example, regular targets of conservatives for alleged liberal leanings, were just as likely as all other outlets to declare 1980 and 1994 conservative mandates.

It is often noted that one gets pretty much the same news – if not in the same depth – from all sources in the United States. This evidence is consistent with that thesis. We surmise that mandate calls are inherently controversial and news organizations want good company when they reach them.

Conclusion by Headline. We have been writing of "explanations" of the vote. These are arguments that appeal to evidence and analysis. News organizations frame such arguments with headlines, capsule summaries of what is to come. For the elite consensus, which is the centerpiece of our theory, argument and analyses are the right level of information flow. Such subtleties – and more – are attended to by professionals in the business of politics.

If instead we were to ask what the general public sees from election coverage, then we know that what it sees is mainly at the level of television, more sound bites than arguments. To get some sense of what the public saw on these three occasions we look at headlines, the frames, not the story. We look to see if bold print carries bold assertions.

Most headlines are not frames, simply facts. The *Times* morning after story about Senate races in 1964 is typical: "3 G.O.P. SENATORS LOSE" (*New York Times*, Nov. 4, 1964). Such plain facts account for about 57 percent of all the headlines in our survey. What then of the other 43 percent? Of them, the most important thing we know is that they tend strongly to support the mandate interpretation. The *Times*, on the same day as its neutral Senate headline, said of the presidential contest, "WHAT GOLDWATER LOST: VOTERS REJECTED HIS CANDIDACY, CONSERVATIVE CAUSE AND THE G.O.P." (*New York Times*, Nov. 4, 1964). Later, the *Times* said it all in a single word title: "MANDATE" (*New York Times*, Nov. 18, 1964). Sixteen years later, it did not pull its punch on the conservative mandate of the

Republican win of presidency and Congress, writing, "REAGAN BUOYED BY NATIONAL SWING TO RIGHT; POSITION BOLSTERED BY G.O.P." (Nov. 6, 1980) and "CONGRESS: TIME FOR ALL GOOD LIBERALS TO COOL IT" (Nov. 9, 1980). Or, again in 1994, "A HISTORIC REPUBLICAN TRIUMPH: GOP Captures Congress; Sharp Turn to Right Reflects Doubts About Clinton, Democrats" (Nov. 9, 1994) or "THE 1994 ELECTIONS: VOTERS; 'It's Like a Call to Arms, Which the Democrats Will Ignore at Their Peril'" (Nov. 10, 1994).

Of those headlines that included some sort of explanation in the bold print, about 80 percent supported the mandate conception. That gives us a sense of why the public should believe in mandates; it is very directly told that they exist. But does the public matter in this matter of interpreting its own motives? We don't know, but speculate that public belief adds to the head of steam of the mandate consensus.

Partisan Explanations. If news sources don't differ much on the election story, a fairly strong difference can be found on the sources cited in news stories. Partisan sources, in particular, appear with some frequency and offer an interesting pattern of first agreement and later disagreement on what the election meant.

We classify sources by whether they are of the winning or losing party in the particular election.[14] We ask if they tell the same story of what happened. The answer is that they do not. Figure 2.8 highlights the partisan difference. It shows that the winners turn almost exclusively (91 percent) to mandate and issue explanations of their win. Those from the losing side split almost evenly (fifty-two to forty-eight) in their assessments. This is not a great surprise. But when we turn next to looking at how it plays out over time, it will turn out to be a more complicated matter.

2.4.1 Explanation Dynamics

As earlier in this chapter, we are interested not only in interpretation but also in its dynamics, how election explanations emerge over time,

---

[14] In most cases, the classification is easy and obvious; the sources are elected officials, party leaders, campaign consultants, and the like. In a handful of cases, for example, labor leaders, one needs to know that they are not neutral players in politics.

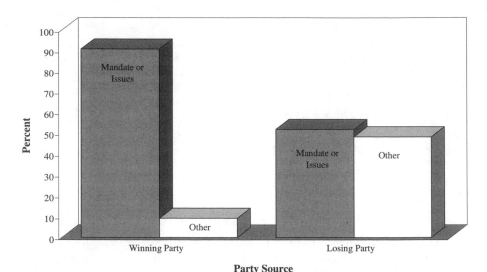

FIGURE 2.8. Election Explanations by Winning and Losing Partisans.

some gaining support and some losing. The topic naturally divides itself into two components, the morning after – actually the days after – and then the emergence of consensus over the full period between election and the seating of the new Congress.

The Morning After. In the immediate aftermath of the sweeping outcome journalists need sources who will say something appropriate to the facts just witnessed. Winners predictably – too predictably – will appreciate the extent of the victory. It makes better news for those from the losing side to concede the loss. And after a sweep the usual, "we're reasonably pleased with the outcome" best face won't do. An unusual result requires total concession.

Total concession is what we see early after election night. Reacting to the election called by the *Times*, the "... greatest popular mandate in American history" (Nov. 15, 1964), Everett Dirksen, Senate minority leader in 1964, "conceded [that]he had expected a tough campaign, but 'I did not expect a typhoon'" (*New York Times*, Dec. 12, 1964).

Sixteen years later, in 1980, it would fall to Democrats to concede natural disaster. "A tidal wave hit us from the Pacific, the Atlantic, the Caribbean and the Great Lakes," House Speaker Thomas P. (Tip) O'Neill conceded (*US News and World Report*, Nov. 24, 1980).

Nor was the 1980 verdict left as a mere Republican win. Ohio Democratic chairman Paul Tipps said,

The election tells me one thing. That is that any public figure who is a liberal Democrat had two choices: find another job or change his philosophy. (*Washington Post*, Nov. 6, 1980)

"What we saw," Pat Caddell, Jimmy Carter's pollster added,

was a massive protest vote directed against the in party.... We've known for a long time there's been a lot of frustration and anger out there. Finally, a lot of people said, "I've had enough and I'm not going to take any more."

The 1994 contest was much the same as 1980, with Democratic leaders conceding not merely defeat, but electoral dominance by their opponent Republicans. The chairman of the Democratic National Committee, David Wilhelm, told the *New York Times*,

Well, we made history last night. Call it what you want: an earthquake, a tidal wave, a blowout. We got our butts kicked. We're bruised and battered, but we're still standing. (*New York Times*, Nov. 10, 1994)

This view was echoed by other prominent Democrats:

"Obviously, what happened last week was disastrous from coast to coast," Don Sweitzer, political director of the Democratic National Committee, told the Association of State Democratic Chairs at the start of a two-day meeting. "It was a wave." (*Washington Post*, Nov. 11, 1994)

Thus begins consensus. A convincing win, mandate claims by the winners, concessions by the losers. That's what it takes. It doesn't happen often. But when it does, the verdict becomes official. The election carried a message. All should heed it. And then it begins to unravel.

Defending the Message. Conceding a loss is easy. In these unusual elections in which one party is winning everything and one losing everything, the loss is just a plain fact. Conceding the interpretation is another matter. To concede that voters rejected the party for its message is very hard. For if the message truly has been renounced, why should the party that carries it continue to exist? Where commitment to democracy is deeply ingrained, then admission that a majority of thoughtful voters has rejected the essence of the party calls for searching reappraisal.

In this light, we expect parties to rise to the defense of their raison
d'etre, to defend the message. And defend it they do. After the first
week or so, party leaders from the losing side begin to go on record
with alternative explanations of the election, explanations, often clever,
that don't call into question the party's basic views.

In 1964, the drift of defending the message was to isolate the Gold-
waterites from the mainstream of the Republican party and argue that
the party itself didn't lose, only the Goldwater faction. The *Times* itself
started the claim on the morning after, with votes still being counted:

Republican candidates for the House and Senate and for governorships across
the country have paid a high price for their party's irresponsibility in nominating the Goldwater-Miller ticket. (Nov. 4, 1964)

Republican moderates, those who had supported the candidacies
of Rockefeller, Lodge, Scranton, or – always in the wings – Richard
Nixon, began a two-month campaign of attacking the Goldwater control of the Republican Party. Jacob Javits's views were typical:

Millions of American who voted for President Johnson did so not in enthusiasm
over his policies, but in protest against the version of Republicanism offered
in the name of the Goldwater-Miller ticket. (*New York Times*, Nov. 15, 1964)

But concession didn't come from all wings of the party. Under attack
from moderates in their own party for losing the election, conservative
Goldwater backers discovered that the electoral glass was half full.
Goldwater's 39 percent of the national vote represented twenty-six
million votes, a high-water mark for a "true conservative" candidate.[15]
They claimed to be celebrating a historic turning point.

The press turned naturally to defeated President Jimmy Carter for
an explanation of the 1980 outcome. He saw it as normal politics, not
the mandate that Ronald Reagan claimed:

But in the end, the president said, the key factor "was just a frustration that
there are some unresolved challenges and problems, and the natural tendency is
to vote against incumbents in the U.S. Senate, the Congress and the presidency."
(*Washington Post*, Nov. 6, 1980).

---

[15] What the arithmetic mainly shows is that any comparison of absolute vote totals
to the smaller electorate of the era of Harding, Coolidge, and Hoover, the reference
point for true conservatism, is likely to favor the present over the past. The same logic
makes the 1972 McGovern totals and then the 1984 Mondale showing high water
marks for "true liberals."

A Democratic labor leader added a similar sentiment, defending the message, "Economic issues decided the election – not conservative issues" (*US News and World Report*, Nov. 17, 1980).

In 1994, Bill Clinton first conceded the message and later turned to a performance explanation, quoted earlier, saying that the economic recovery under his first two years had not been fast enough or gone far enough. Other Democrats pointed to Clinton himself. "The vote was anti-government, anti-Congress, anti-Democratic and anti-Bill and Hillary Clinton," said a former Democratic member of Congress (*Washington Post*, Nov. 20, 1994). Or Democrats could and did dismiss the whole outcome as a result of low turnout.

Turning away from specific claims and counterclaims, we ask if there is a pattern in mandate assertion and denial over the postelection period. To answer that, we look at the proportions of each of the parties asserting or denying message. Merging our three election content analyses together, we wish to observe how winners and losers behave over time. Because stories about the election are unevenly spaced, about half the first week and then the rest spaced out over the remaining eight weeks, we construct an unusual time series that is daily for the first seven days and then weekly thereafter.

In Figure 2.9, we examine the evolution of support and opposition over time. Winners in the figure behave pretty uniformly, asserting

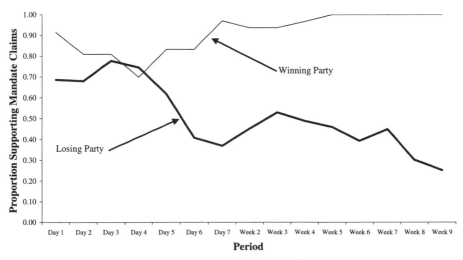

FIGURE 2.9. Support and Opposition to Mandate Claims over Time, by Party of Story Source (Three Period Moving Average).

a mandate for their win almost all the time.[16] The losers are more interesting. First conceding, probably because they have no choice in a dramatic aftermath, they then strategically regroup and begin to deny that the election meant anything.

By the time of the new Congress in January the losing party has a new story, a story of turnout, economics, disunity, candidate mistakes, and the like, all of which have in common that they can explain the election outcome without recourse to willful voters. But consensus, once formed, does not easily yield. And the new story doesn't make much dent in the momentum of mandate talk. It will in time. But that is the story of the next chapter, in which we ask what happens when the new Congress begins its work.

---

[16] And many of the alternative explanations come from people like campaign managers and pollsters who are not so much denying a mandate as asserting that other things – by and large things they controlled – mattered.

3

Members of Congress Respond

In 1981, the two representatives from Dade County, Florida, Democrats Claude Pepper and Dante Fascell were quite similar. Both had held their seats since at least 1963. Both were more in line with the Northern wing of the party than with Southern Democrats, although since 1968 Fascell was as least as, if not more, liberal than Pepper according to the ADA. They both won reelection by relatively large margins. Pepper received 75 percent of the vote, whereas Fascell won 65 percent. In 1980, they voted together 92 percent of the time. Their districts, in addition to being contiguous, were also quite similar. By 1981, Dade County was becoming increasingly Cuban (a trend continued through the 1980s), and both districts were becoming less Democratic. In 1976, both districts gave majorities to the Democratic candidate Jimmy Carter, Pepper's district giving Carter 56 percent of its vote, Fascell's giving 53 percent. In 1980, both districts went for Republican Ronald Reagan with an identical 55 percent of the vote.

The similarity gave way to difference on one particularly important vote. On May 7, 1981, the House of Representatives took its final vote on the budget reconciliation bill. This single vote was the broad blueprint of the Reagan revolution. It deliberately tied the hands of the Congress later in that session by forcing large cuts in spending and taxes. It was an unprecedented scaling back in the size of the federal government, essentially representing the entire Reagan revolution in a single up or down vote. These two members, alike in so many ways, split their votes. This is not unheard of, but it was rare – in the previous year, they split only 8 percent of the time. What makes this split a little more unusual, however, is that it is the more liberal Fascell who supported the conservative bill, while Pepper voted nay.

The explanation for why Fascell voted aye and Pepper nay, we believe, lies in one important difference between the two representatives in early 1981: the *change* in their margins of victory. Although they both easily won reelection, the trend in their votes went in opposite directions. Despite Republican gains in most places, Pepper saw his margin of victory increase from an already safe 63 percent. Fascell, in contrast, saw his share of the vote shrink from 74 percent of the vote to 65 percent. To make matters worse, Fascell faced the same opponent, Herbert Hoodwin, in both elections. Hoodwin's campaign spending in 1980 was less than half the amount he spent in 1978, whereas Fascell increased his spending by more than 50 percent. Thus, despite facing the same candidate and gaining a strong edge in campaign spending (Hoodwin had outspent him two years earlier) Fascell saw his margin of victory shrink from 74–26 to 65–35. Although this would still be considered a "safe" seat (one he would hold until 1992), the change was likely to have caught his attention. He spent more money against the same opponent and yet fared worse.

It does not require much imagination to suggest that Fascell saw this as a signal from his constituents. The obvious message he could take from these election results is that his district was changing. It was becoming more Republican and, presumably, more conservative. This change, as we noted in the previous chapter, was the leading explanation for the national election outcomes, but the message Dante Fascell received from his constituents probably brought this home to him more clearly than for Claude Pepper. Fascell saw a possible shift to the right both nationally and among his constituents. If he cared about his electoral future, he should take signals of electoral change seriously, and here was a clear message that things had changed. The rightward shift that swept Reagan into office was mirrored by a change in his district. His constituents' preferences had changed.

And how would we expect him to react? If he did perceive a rightward move by his constituents, and he believed that this shift was permanent (and thus relevant for future elections), his response is easily predictable. He should move to the right. His voting in Congress should have become more conservative than it would have been without receiving this signal from his constituents. Moreover, although all elected officials would have seen the national signals from the election result, those who also saw a corresponding change in their electoral fortunes (Fascell) should have reacted more and for a longer period of time than those who did not (Pepper). This is precisely what Fascell did. At the start of the session, he voted a more conservative line than we would expect given his past behavior.

This difference, however, might be short-lived. The driving force, we believe, behind Fascell's changing vote patterns was his perception of the state of public opinion in the nation and, more important, in his district. This perception, however, would be fluid. Just as Fascell probably perceived a message in the election returns, members of Congress also receive messages from their constituents to revise these perceptions.

In the previous chapter, we noted that the prevailing meaning of these elections was immediately and decisively linked to claims of a mandate. During the session, the construction of the mandate is largely torn down. Over the course of the 97th session, the conventional wisdom slowly shifted from a "mandate" to a return to regular politics. If Fascell's policy votes were influenced by the current interpretation of public opinion, there should be evidence of a similar evolution in this voting record. His conservative voting should, over time, give way to a more normal, for him, liberal, record of votes.

Dante Fascell, we will assert, was not unique. Given the shared conceptions and constructions of public opinion, it is likely that a sizable proportion of members of Congress are likely to demonstrate a similar behavior – changing their voting patterns to reflect changing assessments of constituent demands. Moreover, who is likely to respond to these changes, which members are more likely to react to signals from the electorate and for how long is also predictable. In this chapter, we demonstrate both that many members respond to the constructions of mandates, and that those who receive the strongest messages are the ones most likely to respond.

3.1 MANDATED CONGRESSES?

Our argument is that members of Congress sometimes perceive elections to be mandates, signals of change in the preferences of their constituents. They react to these perceptions by changing their policy voting in the direction of the perceived change. This reaction, although relatively short-lived, has important consequences.

The extant understanding of congressional decision making lends little guidance as to the specific question of the likelihood of mandate effects. The spatial voting literature, most recently advanced in the work of Poole and Rosenthal (1997), argues that an ideological – that is, liberal/conservative – continuum best accounts for the voting decisions of members of Congress. Other scholars give more attention to electoral forces. The theories vary from Mayhew's (1974) depiction of members as "single minded seekers of reelection" to Arnold's (1990) view that reelection concerns dominate other goals such as good public policy or influence within Congress.

Two lines of research within the congressional decision making literature support the idea that members respond to public opinion and electoral messages. Fenno (1978) and Kingdon (1981), relying on interviews with incumbents, find that members willingly express concern over the potential electoral consequences of their policy decisions. Those studying the link between constituency opinion and legislative decision making often find congruence between the two (Hill and Hurley 1999). Research into the dynamics of representation supports the idea that policy choices by members of Congress are best viewed as an attempt to reconcile constituent, global, and personal preferences with the voting decision at hand (Stimson, MacKuen, and Erikson 1995; Wood and Hinton Andersson, 1998). Elections are thus portrayed as a force that moves representatives toward citizens' preferences.

Direct literature on mandates and congressional voting patterns is quite limited. Two works that do address this issue are openly dismissive. Both Weinbaum and Judd (1970) and Fiorina (1989) address the general question and conclude that the policy effects occur not because members of Congress change their individual voting patterns in response to the election, but simply because of member replacement. The composition of the Congress changes, not the perceptions of members. These authors explicitly assume that the effects of the mandate, if present, will endure, altering the vote patterns for the entire session. After all, if the effect is driven by the changing composition of the chamber, this will not change until the next election. These works do not consider, and their evidence does not speak to, mandate effects that are dynamic, dramatic effects in the early weeks of a Congress that decay to nothing long before its end. Before we can proceed further, we develop such a model.

3.1.1 A Model of Member Response

We presume that members of Congress are reelection seekers. We postulate that their voting is a strategic accommodation of the conflicting demands to satisfy the median voter of their reelection constituency, on the one hand, and the more ideological party base (and quite likely their own policy views), on the other. They attend to news about public opinion and use it to form estimates of where the political center will lie in elections to come. This parallels Stimson, MacKuen, and Erikson's (1995) theory of dynamic representation. Like them, we see politicians using information about public preferences contained in public opinion and election returns to form a perceived expediency position, a position that balances policy interests with electoral security.

In normal times the accommodation of these conflicts will produce an equilibrium voting strategy, a position along the major left-right axis of American politics that is not too far from (probably moderate) district opinion nor so moderate as to dishearten the faithful. The "news" of a mandate is more important than routine observation of public opinion because evidence of apparent electoral impact of changing opinion carries with it a powerful signal about the relevance of opinion change. To interpret the usual signal about opinion change, the politician must ask, "What is the change?" and "will it actually affect votes?" Both, but particularly the latter, require discounts for uncertainty. The policy mandate message stands apart from the norm because it is decisive, asserting both opinion change and electoral relevance in one capsule. Of equal importance is the nature of the message contained in the socially constructed mandate. It is as general as it is decisive. Public opinion rarely crystallizes on specific issues in such a way that members can draw on it to inform specific votes (Stimson 1991; Stimson, MacKuen, and Erikson 1995). As a result, the information that matters is general information, information that a sizable portion of the electorate wants more or less government activity. Perceived mandates offer such information.

Members of Congress do not behave as if they are invulnerable to electoral defeat. Congressional scholars believe quite the contrary. They see current members as "running scared" because they subscribe to the idea that they are, to borrow Mann's (1978) phrase, "unsafe at any margin" (Erikson 1976; Jacobson 1987). This belief is attributed to the development of a more candidate-centered electoral politics. Jacobson (1987) notes that a more candidate-centered electorate may develop a more personal attachment to an incumbent, but it also may be more fickle. The personal hold an incumbent develops is, he argues, as easy to lose as it is to win. In short, an easy win in one year does not guarantee reelection. Congressional behavior, both on the chamber floor and on the campaign trail, is strongly rooted in the electoral connection. As the strategic politician theory suggests, this behavior also may be directed at warding off stronger challengers down the road (Jacobson 1987). Incumbents have taken on the responsibility of ensuring their own reelection, a responsibility that probably drives their response to the Washington community's interpretation of election results.

When that interpretation signals a mandate, the expected response of the rational politician is to rethink the equilibrium voting strategy. If politics has changed, then the assumptions about future electoral threats and opportunities also must change. And whether the politician is happy or dismayed with the election result, the change will be in the direction of the perceived mandate. Members of the disadvantaged party will find themselves likely to be further away from the center than before and therefore face new pressure to moderate. Ideological moderation is increasingly seen as a factor in shaping public opinion and voting behavior (Alesina et al. 1993; Mebane 2000; Zaller 1998). To those on the losing end, mandates are a strong signal that the middle may have shifted. Members of the advantaged party will be emboldened by the new evidence of electoral support for their preferred positions. If the broader electorate is moving in their direction there should be little consequence to moving toward a more extreme position, especially as it is closer to their primary constituency. For both groups, the magnitude of the mandate response may be mitigated by electoral experience or by the security of an ideologically homogenous constituency, but even the most secure incumbent cannot afford to lose touch lest he or she become the victim of the next big electoral surprise.

3.1.2 Reconstructing Mandates

But this construction of what the election was about and what the state of public opinion is changes. Assuming that members care about public opinion implies that they pay close attention to how opinion changes. We previously have suggested that the press is the proper stage to seek constructions of mandates. In Chapter 2, we demonstrated how the meaning of an election is constructed between election night and the start of the congressional session. Here we repeat this analysis, only focusing on how these elections and public opinion more generally are reconstructed during the session.

The availability of electronic archives of media coverage allows us to have a complete depiction of the media coverage of the 1981 and 1995 sessions of Congress. We analyzed the coverage in the *New York Times*, *Washington Post*, *Associated Press*, and *Universal Press International*, looking for how the media depicted the election after seeing how the president and Congress responded. For 1965, we are limited by the availability of data and can only examine the coverage of the *New York Times*. The design continues the analysis of the previous chapter – counting the number of stories depicting or denying the election as a mandate over the first year of the congressional session.

Figure 3.1 presents the patterns of media coverage during the 1981 and 1995 sessions. For each year, we generate a cumulative count of the number of stories promoting or denying a mandate in the previous election. The solid line reports the pattern for 1981 and the dashed line reports the trend for 1995. With the cumulation beginning on the morning after election day, both series start off in consensus territory. In 1981, the early messages are largely balanced, but they drop off precipitously in September undermining the mandate consensus. The depiction of the 1994 elections begins with a pro-mandate slant, reflecting hype about a "first one hundred days" to come, but that erodes rapidly through March and April, with consensus disappearing by August. Although the data for 1965 are scant (too scant to include in the figure), a slightly different pattern holds. Early in the session, the election gets spun as more of a repudiation of Goldwater than a mandate for Johnson. As the session progresses, the pro-mandate media messages pick up some, suggesting that Johnson's success is partially attributable to the signal the voters sent the previous November.

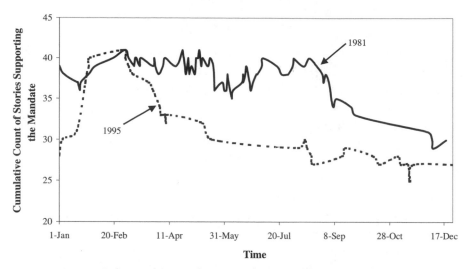

FIGURE 3.1. Balance of Pro- and Antimandate Press Mentions, 97th and 104th Sessions of Congress. (Source: Compiled by the authors from the *New York Times,* the *Associated Press, United Press International,* and *Washington Post.*)

3.1.3 1965

These overall patterns show the general trends in the depictions of the mandates, but the images evoked in the language make the point clearer. The language used to describe the 1964 election actually became somewhat more supportive of the mandate interpretation, at least early in the session. The early depictions combined the mandate interpretation with an emphasis on the poor candidacy of Goldwater, and the vestiges of Kennedy's popularity. As Johnson implemented large portions of the Great Society while maintaining his popularity, the focus began to shift toward a singular focus on the mandate. In his piece written on inauguration day, Tom Wicker of the *New York Times* suggested that the success Johnson will see in office is "aided by his election victory and the shattering of the Republican Party, as well as by his huge majorities in Congress..." (*New York Times,* Jan. 20, 1965, p. 22). Once these successes began to occur, the emphasis on Goldwater diminished. In April, Wicker would begin to revise these views:

[F]ew observers here believe Mr. Johnson is likely to begin fumbling and stumbling, no matter what misfortunes befall. No small part of his success has been due to circumstances beyond his efforts – the national prosperity he inherited, for instance, and the opportunity to run against Mr. Goldwater. Even so, Lyndon Johnson has given ample proof that he is no longer just a political accident in the White House. He knows what he is doing and how to do it, as few presidents have. (*New York Times*, Apr. 18, 1965, p. E3)

In the same article, Wicker suggests that Vietnam is the only possible threat to Johnson's standing and his success in carrying out his mandate.

In early July, things began to change. The United States became involved in a confusing and volatile situation in the Dominican Republic. Vietnam began to heat up, and the press began criticizing Johnson. These foreign involvements lead several commentators to criticize Johnson as they had not previously. Walter Lippman, quoted in the *New York Times*, suggested that Johnson's Vietnam policy would lead the country to a choice "between the devil of unlimited war and the deep blue sea of defeat" (*New York Times*, July 11, 1965, p. E1). Moreover, the *New York Times* also suggested that

some of the blight [from foreign affairs] spread to domestic matters as well, and last week as editorialists, columnists and others toted up the pluses and minuses, one thing was at least clear: the Johnson honeymoon was threatening to become a misty memory.

This criticism was short-lived. The Dominican situation was resolved and by early August, the Johnson mandate was revitalized. In reviewing the first several months of 1965 and previewing the near future, the *New York Times* referred to Johnson's success as a

political miracle. It even surpassed his [Johnson's] own expectations, which were not modest and while he's a long way from achieving a Great Society, he is at least making progress toward a more equal and compassionate society. (*New York Times*, Aug. 6, 1965, p. 26)

These policy changes, however, were not merely the result of the collapse of the Republicans or the Kennedy legacy but also a call for liberal policy by the voters:

The New Deal's day has finally come. The radical ideas of the early thirties are now winning instead of losing. There seems to be a new sense of social responsibility in the country – a growing feeling that racial discrimination, bad education, inadequate medical care and degrading poverty are intolerable in a fabulously wealthy nation.

Democrats were not the only ones reacting to this perception of change. On civil rights at least, Republicans were not only following Johnson, but were at times leading the charge for equal civil rights.

The coverage from 1965, then, presents a clear picture of the mandate. Although skeptical early on, the media turned to fully support the mandate claims. Whereas a few foreign policy troubles would lead some to doubt Johnson's mandate, the domestic policy success, and Johnson's continued popularity would lead some to develop a picture of the American public as clearly calling for a move to the left.

3.1.4 1981

The 1981 coverage is a different pattern. The evolution of the mandate construction in 1981 is probably made clearest by focusing on the writings of a single columnist over the course of the session. On inauguration day, 1981, Tom Wicker of the *New York Times* in an article entitled "Mandate and Burden" compared Reagan's position, both in terms of the support he received and the size of the attempted policy change to Franklin Roosevelt, "without the emergency conditions and Congressional majorities that gave FDR virtually a free hand. All Americans will wish their new President well, as he begins the job – but none should expect miracles nor demand success tomorrow" (*New York Times*, Jan. 20, 1981, p. 31A).

By April 10, his tone had changed little. He referred to the Democrats' attempts to offer an alternative budget bill as an

artful package...that roughly meets the mandate of last year's elections and on which moderates and conservatives may possibly stand together. Perhaps more important, it demonstrates that neither the assumptions nor the details of the Reagan economic proposals are sacrosanct and that the President's stated goals can be reached by other – in some cases better – means than those he has so confidently laid out. (*New York Times*, Apr. 10, 1981, p. 31A)

Although the opposition was starting to grow, the election of 1980 was still clearly a mandate. In early June, Wicker began to equivocate, referring to Reagan as "a president who can reasonably claim he's trying to carry out an election mandate... " (*New York Times*, June 2, 1981, p. 15A). This places the mandate as contestable rather than factual, but still sees the mandate claims as reasonable. By this point, the foundations of the Reagan revolution had been created. The budget blueprint, the tax cuts, and the increases in defense spending had been passed.

Wicker, by the end of July, sees things as changing with Reagan's attempts at changing civil rights and social policy "stretching Mr. Reagan's mandate to its limits, if not going beyond them..." (*New York Times,* July 31, 1981, p. 23A). The mandate perception still exists, it is merely that Reagan has begun to go too far. By September, Wicker pushes it further. By this time, Reagan and Congress have moved to the spending allocations and are debating bills cutting welfare spending, aid to cities, and job training. Wicker asked

Is this what the American people voted for in 1980? Is Mr. Reagan really carrying out a "mandate" when he decides to defer retirees' cost-of-living increases (at an average three-month cost to Social Security recipients of $87 and to veterans of $94) in the very teeth of his own pledges not to cut these benefits? Few people, certainly not a majority of Americans, voted for such specifics as that – or for cutting schoolchildren's bread servings from eight to one a week, or for slashing mine safety inspection funds. Rather, the people voted to "give his program a chance" in its main outlines." (*New York Times,* Sept 23, 1981, p. 21A)

Here we see the true beginnings of Wicker denying the mandate. It was for a general program and not for these specific cuts. The president has gone too far. The public does not support what he is now trying to do. In short, the mandate is over. What Reagan is attempting to do is too much, too far to the right, and out of step with the American public.

3.1.5   1995

Although the general pattern of coverage in 1995 is similar, there does not appear to be the same evolution within the writings of a single columnist. Still, the language differences between early and late 1995 are striking. In early 1995, writers were hailing the gains made by Republicans as a clear signal of a mandate. One op-ed in the *Washington Post* explicitly argued that the 1994 election was "a 'critical election,' one that changes – indeed reverses – the relation of political parties to the American electorate" (*Washington Post,* Feb. 17, 1995, p. A25).

Keeping with the critical election notion, it is suggested that this mandate was permanent and would shape the 1996 presidential election outcome:

The conventional wisdom to the effect that the Republican Party will now have to move to the "center" if it is to retain its majority has it all wrong. What it fails to recognize is that 1994 was an ideological election. What the party must do now is to recognize that it is the center and govern appropriately.... It does not so much matter who the [1996] Republican candidate is as whether he will be willing to ratify the popular mandate the party has been awarded.

In other words, not only was 1994 a mandate for conservative policy but also the change that it signaled was permanent. It was clearly going to last through the next election cycle – the one most relevant to all sitting members of Congress.

During these early days of the session, even skeptics such as Robert Samuelson of the *Washington Post* were supportive of the idea that the public's wishes had changed between 1992 and 1994. "In November, voters may not have endorsed an explicit 'contract' or created a detailed 'mandate.' But they surely desired a shift in direction" (*Washington Post,* Jan. 4, 1995, p. A15). Thus, the consensus construction of the election of 1994 was a rightward shift in the minds of the voters.

The reconstruction of the 1994 mandate began earlier. The claims of overreaching the mandate began as early as the beginning of March as Newt Gingrich discussed dismantling the federal school lunch program. This action led one *Washington Post* editorialist to suggest that,

by such overreaching, such high-C rhetoric, Gingrich and his band of demolition experts are in danger of squandering the mandate they had to reform – not trash – government in Washington. (*Washington Post,* Mar. 9, 1995, p. A21)

Again, the language still suggests that a mandate was to be found in the election results, but that the leadership had overstepped this call for action.

By May, even that would change. Instead, the Republican's claims of mandates were being discounted altogether. "Republicans, in a grand bluff, have interpreted their narrow November 1994 House and Senate wins as a sweeping mandate for radical change. But you'd never know it from the polls" (*Washington Post,* May 22, 1995, p. A23). By November, the revisionist view was complete. E. J. Dionne argued that,

After 1994, the Republicans acted as if they suddenly had a mandate from heaven and the voters to do anything they wanted. But what mandate? The Republicans gathered roughly 52 percent of the vote in the House elections. The turnout was 39 percent of the potential electorate, hardly a popular outpouring. Their new majorities in both houses were quite narrow. And the evidence is quite clear that the 1994 vote was more a negative verdict on the Democrats' failures than the result of some sharp ideological turn in the public. (*Washington Post,* Nov. 14, 1995, p. A19)

Even conservative pundit William Kristol claimed that the actions taken by Congress were a mistake. Instead of pushing their conservative agenda as quickly as they did, the Republicans should have taken "incremental steps to build toward a real mandate in 1996 that would give them both the institutional and popular support to achieve their program" (quoted by Dionne, Nov. 14, 1995, p. A19).

3.1.6 A Reconstructed Mandate

In sum, we see a similar pattern in all three years. The early discussion of the election in the media and, we believe, the Washington community more generally, supported the consensus construction of the election as a mandate. As government acted, as it passed (at least partially in the case of 1995) legislation that would move policy in the direction of the mandate, the discussion changed. As the focus moved from broad changes in the direction of policy to specific, usually unpopular changes, the descriptions changed. Commentators and, presumably, politicians began to fear that the mandate party was overstepping the mandate.

By the end of the congressional session, the reconstruction of the election would be complete. These elections, in the end, were not calls for grandiose change in public policy. They were not declarations of support for the winning party. They were not, in short, mandates. They were repudiation of the previous policies or candidates. The public wanted, it was believed by the end, change, but not the change the mandate parties were giving it.

3.1.7 Mandate Dynamic and Mandate Response

To this point we have suggested two things. Members react to their perceptions of public opinion, and these perceptions change rapidly and dramatically during the session after a mandate. Together, these imply that the policy voting equilibrium of members of Congress is dynamic. Members should move away from their old equilibrium at the outset of the new Congress because of the strong construction of a mandate perception. As the mandate is reconstructed, their voting pattern should decay back to the normal equilibrium. The recalculation of their electorally expedient position causes the dynamics. As the consensus of a mandate erodes, the factors that produced normal member equilibria in the first place reassert themselves.

The expected dynamic response is pictured in Figure 3.2. It shows a hypothetical member's equilibrium and our expectation of an early deviation toward a conservative mandate that eventually dissipates as the election becomes ever more distant over time. The mechanism behind this change, we believe, is the evolving construction of the meaning of the previous election. Although the picture here is a smooth impulse-decay pattern, the actual rate of the decay should depend on the rate of change in the depiction of the mandate election.

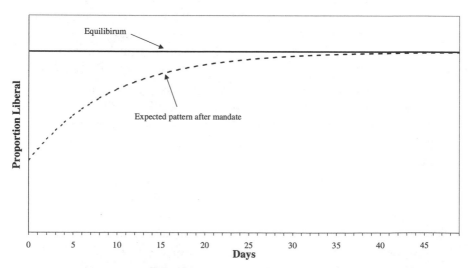

FIGURE 3.2. Expected Member Response to Perception of Conservative Electoral Mandate (Presuming Decaying Consensus of Mandate).

Given this image and expected pattern, we now turn to the task of developing a strategy to uncover change in how members of Congress vote over the course of a session.

3.2 SETTING UP A TEST

To move from theory to test we need a means of observing when the appearance of mandate behavior is present or absent. For data, we have the roll call votes cast by all members of both houses of Congress. What is needed is a means to translate the "yea" or "nay" votes into evidence of mandate influence, present or absent for each member at various points during the session. The conception of the mandate state can be stated simply: *a member is in a mandate state when he or she (1) deviates from personal equilibrium (2) in the direction of the mandate (3) beginning at the start of a session following a mandate election.* That requires that we observe a sequence of votes with clear ideological content and polarity, estimate personal equilibrium positions for each member, and then observe whether a cumulated pattern of votes at the beginning of the session diverges significantly from that equilibrium or not. The result will be a sequence of binary codes in which each member is classified as in the mandate state or not as the session progresses.

3.2.1 Observing Reactions to Mandates

Our strategy for coding the ideological content of the votes is taken from Stimson, MacKuen, and Erikson (1995). It examines each individual roll call to determine if it is ideological and in which direction by mapping the vote distribution onto member ADA scores.[1] A vote is liberal, for example, if members who vote the "yea" position have higher average ADA scores than those voting "nay." The standard employed for "higher" is that the split between "yea" and "nay" must be greater than thirty, which is roughly the ADA split on a pure party vote. When this threshold is not met, we presume that the voting alignment might

---

[1] Because our use of ADA scores is for cross-sectional validation, we use them in their original form, not the "inflation adjusted" version of Groseclose, Levitt, and Snyder (1999).

be accidental with regard to ideology, the leading cause for concern being party against party votes that might have nonideological causes. Our intent in applying the ideological polarization criterion parallels Stimson, MacKuen, and Erikson (1995). We want to ensure we are observing a left-right cleavage when defection from partisanship (in the direction of the mandate) is itself along left-right lines. A further benefit is that a small number of symbolic votes staged for effect by party leaders early in the session will have no influence at all if they do not polarize along the ideological cleavage and little influence, because they are averaged together with others, even if they do.

The goal of this measurement strategy is to reliably identify changes in a member's ideological voting over the course of an entire session. The choice we face is to determine how to aggregate these individual votes into a specific metric. If we analyze this on a vote-by-vote basis, we run the risk of single, idiosyncratic votes mischaracterizing the ideology of the member. For instance, according to this coding scheme, Ted Kennedy cast a single conservative vote in the first year of the 104th session. This vote happened to be the second roll call that we include in our analyses. Given a simple vote-by-vote approach to identifying the dynamics of the member ideology, Kennedy would appear to fit this pattern. After the second vote, his liberalism was 0.5, after the third it was 0.67, the fourth 0.75, and continued to increase, looking similar to the hypothesized depiction in Figure 3.2. But we do not really believe that this demonstrates a reaction to a mandate election. At least, we have little confidence in this conclusion. Thus, we wish to have a longer period of observation to minimize the influence of single votes.

Of course, aggregation has the opposite problem. If mandates are ephemeral, then a high level of aggregation is likely to understate the effects. Weinbaum and Judd (1970), in their unsuccessful effort to find mandate effects in Congress aggregate to a full year. If we are correct that the mandate consensus is likely to erode, and that the vote patterns of members of Congress, are responsive to these changes, then this high level of aggregation will seriously understate the effects of the mandate.

As something of a compromise, we choose to aggregate these ideological roll calls into blocks of ten votes. Each block of ten votes constitutes a legislative period – albeit one that does not map uniformly onto regular units of time. We first estimate each member's personal voting equilibrium, the normal level of support for the liberal alternative in left versus right votes, from the member's behavior at the end of the first session. We then code the member as being in a mandate state if (1) the member was in the mandate state on the previous block (or it is the first block), (2) the member's observed liberalism for the block deviates in the direction of the mandate, and (3) is more than a standard deviation from his or her equilibrium liberalism. Our goal is to classify members as under mandate influence or not. Each of these decisions serves that goal. We restrict classification of deviations from equilibria to consistent early session behavior and to movements in the correct direction. Because we wish to be sure that we are modeling the election effect only, one particularly conservative decision is that mandate states terminate with a block of normal votes, *and may not resume thereafter*. This rule, combined with random variation and a small N, probably causes us to understate the amount of mandate behavior.

Before we can assess deviation from the norm, we must have a means of estimating members' normal voting positions. Doing so with requisite precision is difficult. We have considered three possibilities, estimating from votes in the previous year, estimating from end of session of the current year, and estimating from the subsequent year. The first, the previous year, is an attractive fit to theory, but carries two problems: (1) it is based on a not strictly comparable legislative agenda; and (2) using these estimates leaves us unable to assess the behavior of new members, who are particularly crucial actors. The second strategy poses a circularity problem; the norm from which deviation is assessed is based on some of the same votes that are being observed. This is a conservative bias for our thesis, making the norm very slightly closer to the behavior of the mandate period than it ought to be, and therefore making it more difficult to observe mandate behavior. The third estimation strategy, using the subsequent (even numbered) year, poses the noncomparable agenda issue and a possible liberal bias; the excesses of the first year of a Congress might be "corrected" by movements away from the mandate message in the second year.[2] This bias could produce evidence of mandate effects where none occurred in reality. All of these estimates, although not identical, are very highly correlated. After much experimentation, we have adopted the second method,

[2] This is often believed to have happened in the 89th Congress (1966) and the 104th (1996) and perhaps even in the 97th (1982).

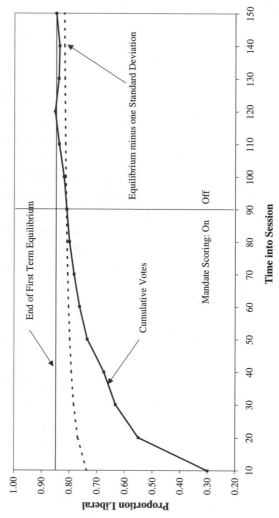

FIGURE 3.3. Mandate Coding for Dante Fascell, 1981.

using end of same session estimates, for our analysis. The circularity issue is very minor and the direction of bias, against our hypotheses, is what good science demands. Alternative coding methods do not in any case alter substantive inferences.

3.2.2 Coding Examples

The coding of mandate behavior for individual members is best understood through examples. Figure 3.3 presents the coding of the representative we began with, Dante Fascell. The solid horizontal line is the end of the first-term equilibrium, the smooth dashed curve is the one standard deviation lower bound of likely chance variation around the equilibrium, and the jagged curve is the actual vote pattern. The width of the area of likely deviation is large at the beginning of the session when there are few votes and grows smaller as evidence accumulates over the session. The vertical line denotes the vote block at which the member returns to equilibrium. For Fascell, this takes place in the ninth vote block, on September 10, 1981.

Figures 3.4 and 3.5 present the same coding information for two Senators from 1981, Paul Tsongas and Gary Hart. The pattern for Tsongas is similar to the one for Fascell. He begins much more conservative than would be expected based on his equilibrium. As the session progresses, his voting pattern approaches his equilibrium liberalism level until the difference is no greater than would be expected by chance, after 80 roll call votes. At this point, June 26, we code Tsongas as having gone back to equilibrium. The mandate effect for him lasted a total of 176 days.

Figure 3.5 presents one other element of our coding rules. As noted earlier, we attempt to take a conservative estimate of when the member of Congress goes back to equilibrium voting. Thus, we code members as having permanently "exited" the mandate state the first time their proportion of liberal votes is less than one standard deviation away from their equilibrium. The coding for Gary Hart demonstrates why this may understate the effects of the mandate. After 140 roll calls (October 22), Hart's vote pattern was slightly more liberal than our cutoff point (the actual liberal proportion is 0.855 while the equilibrium minus one standard deviation is 0.853). Hart proceeded to cast only seven liberal votes in the next ten ideological roll calls. This made his vote pattern drop back below the cutoff point and remains there for

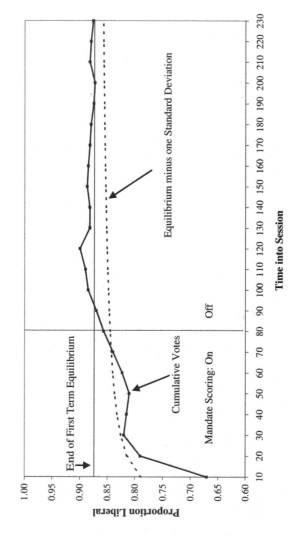

FIGURE 3.4. Mandate Coding for Paul Tsongas, 1981.

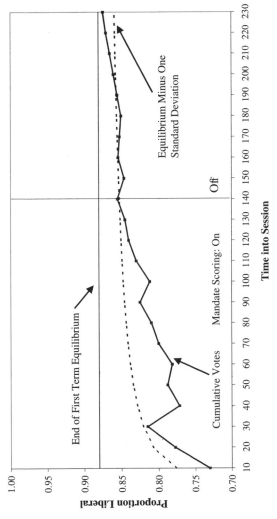

FIGURE 3.5. Mandate Coding for Gary Hart, 1981.

more than one month, until the two hundredth roll call on December 2. Our coding scheme thus results in a much more conservative estimate of the length of time the senator was influenced by the mandate.

We wish to ask, "How long do mandates last?" We now have the appropriate data in hand, sequences for all individual members of the form "oooiiiiiiiiiii..." where the "o's" – standing for ten vote blocks in which the mandate influence is "on" – delimit the period of mandate influence. We also know the day at which the member's voting pattern is no longer distinguishable from what would normally be expected.

3.3 MODELING MANDATES

We are now equipped to identify which members of Congress reacted to these three mandate elections by altering their roll call voting – and for how long. Before we address these two questions (who and for how long), we identify several member characteristics that are likely to introduce heterogeneity into the expected mandate response.

3.3.1 Modeling Individual Behavior

We want to know who alters their voting patterns and who does not, how long lasting is the change, and what sorts of factors enhance or diminish the duration of the effects. All of these questions require a model of duration, using what we know about individual members to predict the dynamics of individual response. To set up that analysis, we turn to thinking about individual differences in response to the presumed mandate.

Our theory to this point applies equally to all members. But it has elements that suggest that some members will react differently to the stimulus of a mandate election. We expect members who have witnessed the most striking electoral effects in their own reelections to respond more strongly, we expect asymmetries of threat along party and ideological lines, and we expect that political experience will moderate response. We detail our expectations for the determinants of the likelihood of reacting immediately following the election and for the length of time of these effects (if they occur). Although similar, the likelihood of responding and the length of time that a member stays affected are different phenomena. The former stems from the strength of the message the member receives. Although all members receive a similar message about national politics, there may be individual differences in their messages. The latter, the length of the mandate effect, probably has more to do with the ability of the member to update his or her perceptions of public opinion. We address what we believe are the determinants of both before modeling them separately.

Electoral Effects. Incumbent members are highly sensitive to the size of their victory margins. Members of either party who witness big differences in the mandate election result should take the evidence more seriously than those who do not. Newly elected members, lacking a baseline of prior election outcomes, may be most inclined to (over) credit their election to the policy attitudes of voters. This will prove hard to model, but the sort of effect that we anticipate is that "out" party members (those who the mandate went against) who just barely survive the election after previously comfortable electoral margins should be most likely to change their behavior. For them, the mandate story is not just opposition rhetoric, it is an immediate threat to their electoral career. It is also highly relevant information about the viability of their normal voting strategy.

This implies an asymmetric impact of changes in electoral margin. Those who do not have a change in their margin of victory should be less affected than those who suffer from large losses or benefit from large gains. If the margin does not change, then there is no clear evidence that the preferences of constituents have moved. These members can afford to be less responsive. Thus, we expect the change in the margin of victory to affect both the likelihood of being affected and the duration of the effect. Members with larger changes in their margin of victory should be more likely to be affected and remain affected longer than members with small changes.

Additionally, we expect members to respond more to losses than gains. Gains can easily be credited to the candidate. He or she simply ran a better campaign. Losses cannot be excused away as easily. Thus, we expect that those who suffer large losses will respond more than those who have large gains. Both should, in turn, respond more than those who see no change.

Party and Ideology. If the center of politics appears to have moved, the change should affect the behavior of politicians on both sides of it. But there is asymmetry in the nature of the threats and opportunities to the parties advantaged and disadvantaged by the mandate. The disadvantaged, or out, party members should sense that their current behaviors may expose them to future electorates more distant from their views, a difference that may have fatal consequences at the polls. If the political world has changed and they are on the wrong side of the change, they should rebalance their positions in line with the new general election constituency. There is little cost to a bit of moderation in the new Congress. If the mandate proves ephemeral, they can revert to more comfortable positions. And if it does not, they set the stage to begin to establish a new and more viable position. (And if they are wrong about the mandate, the initial votes of the new Congress will conveniently be far from voters' recent memories at the time of the next election.)

"In" party members will sense an opportunity for free expression of their views, now seen to be electorally advantaged. With the center moving toward their preferred position, the need to compromise is relaxed. Their threat – more apparent in the long than the short run – comes from runaway ideologues on their own side who, having overinterpreted the electoral message, now demand purity and commitment of all. If the mandate turns out to be temporary, members of the mandate party may be pulled by their primary constituencies into positions which can prove to be costly.

For ideology, we do not believe it matters which side of the mandate members are on. What is likely to shape the mandate response is how far the member is from the center. Moderate members on both sides face difficult choices, often in difficult districts. They feel the full force of the claimed mandate. Facing a greater threat than others, they also have much to gain, for movements in their middling positions are likely to be noticed by the voters. Those on the ideological extremes, in contrast, often represent districts that support their strong positions and have little need to compromise. Their consistent records also would not be easily changed by a few votes early in the session. We expect that moderates are more likely to move toward the mandate and more likely to stay there for some time.

Seniority. We can think of the world as composed of electoral veterans and novices. Although both have the same stake in protecting an electoral future against defeat, we expect a somewhat different reaction. The message of the mandate election is always that the political world has fundamentally changed and will never revert to the old norm.

This message, which appears to be believed for a time, never turns out to be true in the long run. Thus, we think more senior members who have been through it before and knew that it didn't turn out to be true in the past should be less responsive to the current message.

The Consensus Interpretation of the Washington Community. Unlike these earlier factors that discriminate between members, all members participate in a group conversation about the meaning of political events. We postulate that members take readings of public opinion and update them on a frequent basis. Although they have multiple inputs to this updating, some personal such as constituent conversations and chats with colleagues in the cloakrooms, the one public source of information (and often revisionist information) about mandates is commentary and analysis in the media. We turn to this public expression as a means to leverage the question of what information members are likely to encounter. The often-closed circle of conversations inside the beltway insures that what is in the newspapers gets rapid circulation in the political community. The stronger the pro-mandate balance of news coverage, the stronger the member response.

We are ready now to test these hypotheses. Some of them test our theory at the margin; they can be true or false and the core of the theory can still hold. Two are decisive, changes in victory margin and the flow of mandate coverage. Election outcomes are the critical signal of change to the member. And then the flow of postelection interpretation modulates the signal, telling members that it was more or less important than first believed. If these hypotheses fail then our theory cannot dominate other possible interpretations of aggregate voting change in the early session.

3.4 WHO RESPONDS TO MANDATES?

We begin the analysis of how members of Congress respond to mandates with a simple question: Who is affected. Our dependent variable is dichotomous. We code each of the 1,582 members from 1965, 1981, and 1995 as being affected or unaffected by the mandate.[3] The variable

---

[3] This number is less than 1,605 (535 × 3) because not all members voted on enough of these roll calls to be identifiable early in the session or did not serve long enough to get a reliable estimate of the member's equilibrium.

TABLE 3.1. *Member Response to Mandate (Logit Estimates)*

Variable	Coefficient	Robust Standard Error
Gain in Victory Margin	−0.34	0.34
Loss in Victory Margin	0.73[a]	0.36
Seniority (Number of Terms Served)	0.03	0.01
Ideological Extremity (Folded ADA Rating)	−0.03[a]	0.01
Party of the Mandate	0.61[a]	0.13
Chamber (House)	−0.08	0.16
Year (1981)	1.94[a]	0.16
Year (1995)	1.33[a]	0.17
Intercept	−1.51[a]	0.25
N	1,582	

[a] $p < .05$.

tells us whether or not the member is in the mandate state for the first block of ten. Note, the estimates across years and chambers represent the same number of roll call votes (ten), but they do not represent the same amount of time. For 1965, the tenth vote in the House took place on February 18, whereas the tenth vote for the Senate was on February 25. In 1981, the tenth vote in the Senate occurred on March 26, whereas the House took until May 13. In 1995, this ten-vote block ends on January 10 for the Senate and January 20 for the House. Presumably, the differences across chambers and time create a mean difference in the probability of being affected. To account for these differences we include indicators of being a House member and if the observation was from either 1981 or 1995.[4]

We test our hypotheses via a logit analysis, the results of which are presented in Table 3.1. The dependent variable is dichotomous, coded such that members in the mandate state are assigned a one, those who are unaffected a zero. A positive coefficient indicates that higher values on the independent variable make members more likely to be affected by the mandate.

The results are generally supportive of the hypotheses. Whether or not a member reacts to the mandate depends on the change in his or her

---

[4] The media variable tapping the Washington community's current interpretation of the election is not included in this first analysis because it is a constant for each year. It plays a key role when we look at dynamics in the duration analysis to come.

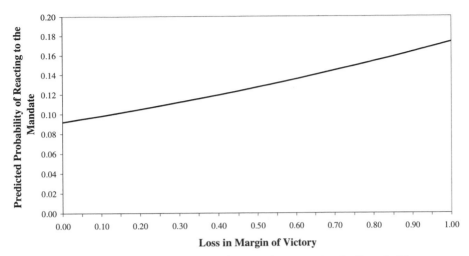

FIGURE 3.6. Predicted Probability of a Mandate Reaction by Loss in Victory Margin.

margin, but only if he or she loses votes. Larger vote losses correspond to a greater probability of reacting to a mandate. The size of a gain in vote margin is unrelated. Additionally, both ideological extremity and the member's partisanship matter. Moderates are more likely to be affected, as are members of the mandate party. Seniority, contrary to our expectation, is unrelated to being affected.

To demonstrate the substantive effects underlying these coefficient estimates, Figures 3.6 and 3.7 present the predicted probability of a member reacting to a mandate over a range of values for the loss in the victory margin and the member's ideological extremity.[5] In both cases, the changes in the predicted probabilities are relatively modest. For the loss in the margin of victory, moving from having no change in one's margin to the fullest possible loss increases the predicted probability of being affected by about 0.08. This is nearly a doubling in the predicted probability. A standard deviation change in the loss of electoral margin (approximately a seventeen-point swing) will increase the likelihood of

[5] As is standard with predicted probability calculations, the other variables need to be assigned some "typical" value. For the graphs in Figures 3.4 and 3.5 the year is set to 1965, party to the nonmandate party, the chamber is the Senate, and seniority is set to eight years. For the margin of victory calculation, the ideological extremity is set to its mean of 34.2. Finally, in the ideological extremity calculation, the change in the margin of victory variables are both set to zero.

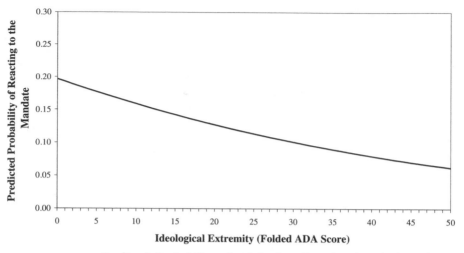

FIGURE 3.7. Predicted Probability of a Mandate Reaction by Ideological Extremity.

being affected by about 0.03 at all of the observed values of the loss in margin.[6]

The ideological extremity graph shows a slightly stronger effect. The most moderate members, those whose ADA scores are fifty, have a one in five chance of being affected by the mandate. At the other end, those who are rated as either perfectly conservative or perfectly liberal have only a one in twenty chance of reacting to the mandate.

In the end, we see that a member's initial decision to respond to the mandate signal is driven primarily by whether his or her party is the victorious one, by his or her ideology, and by the signal sent by the member's own district. This analysis gives us a sense of the factors influencing the first votes taken after the mandate election. To better assess what drives member behavior we now turn to the dynamics of the response.

3.5   DURATION OF MANDATES

Electoral mandates are best understood as dynamic. It is difficult to understand their impact or effects, that is, without reference to time.

---

[6] While the logit model is nonlinear, the specification here is close enough to the midpoint that the impacts of the independent variables are nearly linear.

If a mandate is to have a meaningful effect on behavior or policy, it must change the votes of more than a few legislators and must persist for longer than ten votes.

Before estimating a model of the duration of mandate effects, we look at how the member characteristics of interest to us influence the length of time members are in the mandate state. We begin by looking at how the raw count of members voting in accordance with the mandate changes over time. Figure 3.8 graphs, by the day into the legislative session, the total number of Representatives and Senators who deviate from their normal voting pattern in favor of the given year's mandate.

The figure demonstrates both the differences in the magnitude of the mandate effect across years and the expected impermanence of the changes in individual voting behavior. The Reagan revolution of 1980 stands out as the strongest case. Well into May 1981, fully one quarter of the members of the 97th Congress were voting more conservatively than normal. This is the strong case of mandate voting effects, many members responding and each for a lengthy period of time. The return to old assumptions and old behaviors is equally dramatic. By the end of June, only 11 percent of the members continued in the mandate state.

Although 1995 shows a less pronounced effect than 1981, the 104th Congress still saw close to 20 percent of its members, including nearly a quarter of the Senate, voting more conservatively than we might expect under normal politics. The duration of the effects in 1995 is notable. Nearly 100 members of Congress continued to deviate from their normal pattern well into July. If we add to this the turnover effects brought about by the Republican takeover of Congress, the potential for significant policy change is striking.

The election of 1964 induced the fewest members to alter their voting behavior. In 1965, the potential for a mandate is clearly visible in the year's election returns, when the Democrats gained thirty-seven seats in the House. The strong gains and solidly liberal Democratic majority probably explain the low number of members affected. For many House Democrats, there was little room to their left. The impact of the liberal mandate is more clearly seen in the Senate, where the Democrats picked up two seats in 1964. With turnover effects unlikely to mask the mandate response, we see one quarter of the Senate voting

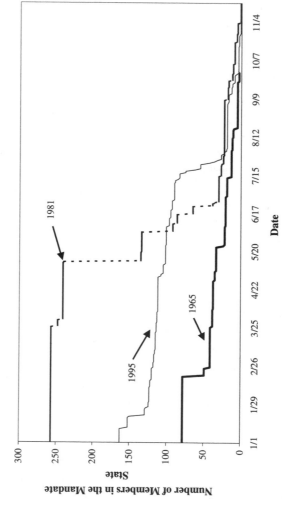

FIGURE 3.8. Number of Members of Congress Who React to the Mandates by Year and Time.

in a more liberal direction through late February and fourteen senators affected by the mandate well into May. A block of fourteen senators, no matter the year, is a potentially powerful force in policy making.

3.5.1 Individual Members and the Mandate Duration

We now turn to our final question: What explains the duration of mandate effects for individual members. We begin with a series of bivariate analyses. Each looks at the percentage of members in the mandate state for each voting block into the session of Congress and combines all three years. We conceptualize behavior as consisting of only two states, voting normally (that is, close to personal equilibria) or deviating in the direction of the mandate, which we label "affected." In each graph, we group the members according to key characteristics in order to get an initial assessment of their influence on the duration of the mandate effect.

We start with Figure 3.9, in which we group members into those who did or did not witness a change in their vote share from the previous election. We expect those whose vote share changed to perceive a greater change in public opinion as a result of the mandate election and to be more likely to deviate from normal behavior. This figure provides

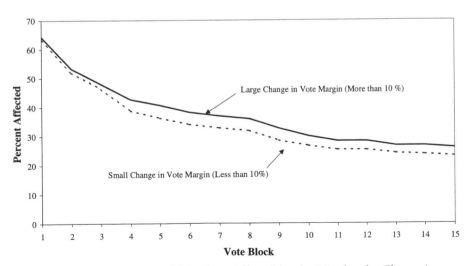

FIGURE 3.9. Percentage of Members Affected by the Mandate by Change in Victory Margin and Time.

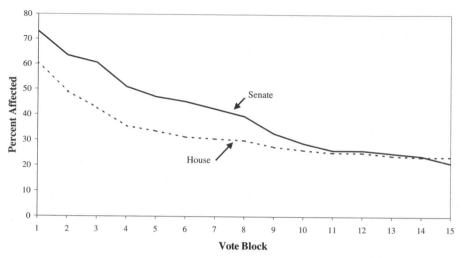

FIGURE 3.10. Percentage of Members Affected by the Mandate by Chamber and Time.

mixed evidence that this is true.[7] In the early periods, when the mandate perception is strongest, there is no difference in the proportion of members still in the mandate state. As the session progresses, however, members who see a small change in vote share return to normal voting more quickly and the proportion remaining in the mandate state is slightly larger for those with a sizable change in their vote share.

In Figure 3.10, we continue to focus on electoral threat, this time looking at behavior across the two houses of Congress. We have no strong priors on chamber differences, but one might expect electoral threat to be stronger in the House where members run continually for reelection. The threat should generally be weaker in the Senate, where members (depending on their election class) have up to six years before their next election. Interestingly, it is the opposite that appears to be true. Senators, not House members, deviate from normal voting for longer periods of time and return more slowly.

---

[7] Note that for these analyses the direction of the effect is whatever the mandate signal was, liberal in 1964 and conservative for the other cases. For the next four figures, the *Y* axes map response to the mandate – in whatever direction it was. Thus, *up* is always toward the mandate signal and *down* is away from it, toward individual member normal behavior.

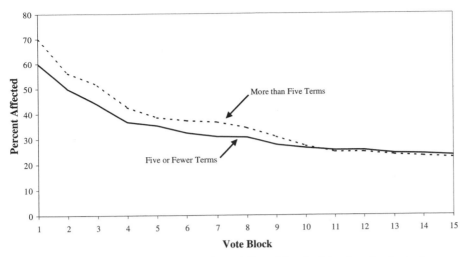

FIGURE 3.11. Percentage of Members Affected by the Mandate by Seniority and Time.

We have postulated that less senior members are more influenced by the mandate phenomenon. Being less likely to have experienced a startling and unexpected election outcome, they may be apt to believe the mandate "spin" and act as if the election foretold a permanent shift in the electorate. More experienced members may have seen such elections before and thus find it easier to discount the perhaps overly strong interpretation of their meaning. In Figure 3.11, we break out incumbents by the number of two year spans they have served – actual terms for members of the House, and an artificial equivalent for Senators. We group them into junior members serving up to their fifth term and more senior members reelected more than five times. The percentage of members affected in each group is very close. What little difference we see suggests that senior members are more likely to respond.

Our expectations about member ideology involve a mix of considerations. Those who are most moderate often are so because they represent heterogeneous and insecure constituencies that will not tolerate more extreme positions. Because these districts mirror the center of politics, the members who represent them should be highly sensitive to messages that suggest the center has shifted. More extreme ideologues, by contrast, have little to gain from a strategic shift of position. Partly because their extremity is often associated with a safe electoral base and

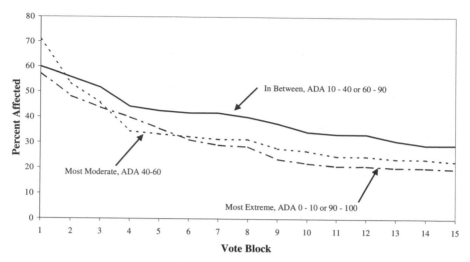

FIGURE 3.12. Percentage of Members Affected by the Mandate by Ideological Extremity and Time.

partly because their claim to moderation lacks credibility, they have less to gain by moving toward the mandate effect in the early session. In Figure 3.12, we break members into three classes from most moderate to most extreme, using a "folded" ADA score (absolute value of actual ADA rating − 50) as our criterion. The most extreme members (ADA scores of 0 to 10 or 90 to 100) are indeed the most likely to return to their normal voting behavior. Surprisingly, the Moderates (ADA between 25 and 75), whereas most likely to respond in the opening set of votes, are affected for a shorter period than those who are in the middle (ADA 10–25 or 75–90).

The complexity of congressional voting behavior ensures that any bivariate analysis is suggestive at best. Moderation, seniority, and victory margins are all interrelated and best studied in a multivariate framework that takes this into account. We turn now to the task of developing and estimating a model that can explain why politicians react for as long as they do. We estimate our model using a logit-based discrete time hazard framework. As is standard with hazard frameworks, we model the probability of exiting a state. The dependent variable is "remains in the mandate state" (scored 0) or "exits the mandate state" (scored 1). This coding is opposite that of the model predicting who is affected. In looking at the initial response, positive coefficients meant that a member is more likely to be affected. In this case, positive effects indicate that the member is more likely to "exit" the mandate state and return to normal. In other words, to be less affected by the mandate.

Recall that the member stays in the mandate state when his or her observed liberalism for the voting block deviates in the direction of the mandate and is more than a standard deviation from his or her equilibrium position. In this analysis, we model the number of days into the session a member is in the mandate state. We do this by taking the number of days into the legislative session that each ten-vote block ends.

3.5.2 Explaining the Different Durations

We now turn to estimating our model of the underlying probability of exiting the mandate state, given that the member was affected in the previous period. Positive coefficients indicate an increasing likelihood of returning to normal politics and thus a shorter mandate effect. Negative coefficients indicate a decreasing probability of returning or a longer mandate effect. The media variable, our measure of the content of the Washington community's perceptions of the election, should be negative – as the pro-mandate media coverage decreases, the probability that a member will exit the mandate state should increase. We expect to find that both gains and losses of victory margin lead members to lengthy deviations from their norm (producing a negative coefficient for both). Seniority should produce a positive coefficient, showing that members that are more senior quickly revert to normal behavior. Ideological extremity should be positive as should party, with members of the mandate party (coded as a 1) being less responsive. The other variables in the analysis (chamber and year dummies) complete the specification and carry no prior expectations.

The estimates of the hazard model are presented in Table 3.2. The probability of exiting the mandate state is heavily influenced by the balance of the media coverage, both gain and loss in reelection margins, ideological extremity, seniority, party, and chamber. Members respond to the messages they receive from both their constituents and the media. The coefficients on all three variables are negative and significant as we predicted. Ideologically extreme members, as expected, show short-lived effects (a coefficient of 0.02). The analysis does not support our expectation of greater out-party effects. The coefficient

TABLE 3.2. *A Full Model of Mandate Duration (Probability of Exiting Mandate State, Given that the Member Is Affected)*

Variable	Coefficient	Robust Standard Error
Balance of Media Coverage	−0.27[a]	0.03
Gain in Victory Margin	−0.91[a]	0.29
Loss in Victory Margin	−0.85[a]	0.30
Seniority (Number of Terms Served)	0.03[a]	0.01
Ideological Extremity (Folded ADA Rating)	0.02[a]	0.00[b]
Party (Party of the mandate)	−0.50[a]	0.14
Chamber (House)	0.79[a]	0.16
Year (1981)	−0.28	0.20
Year (1995)	−1.70[a]	0.19
Time Effect Polynomials		
Polynomial 1	−0.49[a]	0.15
Polynomial 2	0.69[a]	0.12
Intercept	−1.73	0.34
Likelihood Ratio χ^2	723.66	

Note: Polynomials 1 and 2 represent the best fitting fractional polynomials for the hazard function. $N = 5{,}284$.
[a] $p < .05$.
[b] Before rounding, the standard error is 0.004.

(−0.54) is statistically significant but wrong signed; the mandate party remains affected longer than the disadvantaged party. Additionally, the seniority results demonstrate that senior members adapt to the changing information environment more quickly. Finally, the effects of losses and gains are indistinguishable from one another (test of equality, $\chi^2_{1df} = 0.03$, $p > 0.8$). These results, overall, are supportive of the core of our theory but not all of the refinements.

Logit coefficients are inherently difficult to interpret, and their magnitude fails to convey the variables' substantive impact on the length of time the members are affected. For that reason, we again graph a series of predicted probabilities based on changing values of our explanatory variables. The effect of the variable of interest is determined by how much it shifts the probability of exiting away from a baseline probability of exiting. In order to isolate the influence of a single independent variable, we establish a baseline by setting the remaining independent variables to predetermined values. Here the continuous variables are set to their mean, the year is set to 1981, and the chamber is the Senate. We have chosen the media scoring from 1981 to standardize the effect that varies across years. The change in victory margin variables are both set to zero. The party is assumed to be the mandate party.

We begin by examining the effects of the media variable. Predicted probabilities for all other independent variables, because they are constant across time, are easy to calculate. The effect of the time-varying media coverage is more difficult. Our approach is to first calculate the over time predicted probability of a typical member leaving the mandate state given the actual changes in the media coverage from our chosen year (1981). We then calculate the predicted probability for the same member, but keep the content of the media constant across the entire session. The resulting hazard rate, or over time probability of exiting the mandate state, is presented in Figure 3.13.

The effects of the media in Figure 3.13 are quite pronounced. Small changes in the content of the consensus of the Washington community (as reported by the media) result in large changes in the likelihood that a member will return to normal. As the media revisits the previous election and changes the interpretation away from a mandate, members are increasingly likely to return to normal. The large differences between the lines in the middle and at the end of the graph are times when the media are particularly critical of the mandate interpretation.

To properly interpret these numbers, it is important to recognize what the probabilities represent. They are the probability that a member will exit the mandate state on that specific day given that he or she has not exited in the previous period. In 1981, with the media effect included, there is a 10 percent increase in the likelihood of exit for every day between September 5 and the end of the session. At the end of the session, the media effect raised the member's likelihood of exit from a less than one in five chance of reverting to normal behavior to a greater than one in two chance. This sizable effect dampened the mandate and shortened its length considerably.

Figure 3.14 presents a similar analysis demonstrating the impact of changes in a member's electoral margin on his or her reaction to the mandate signal. The line marked "Stable Margin" indicates the predicted hazard rate for a hypothetical member of Congress whose victory margin stayed the same. The "Change in Margin" represents the

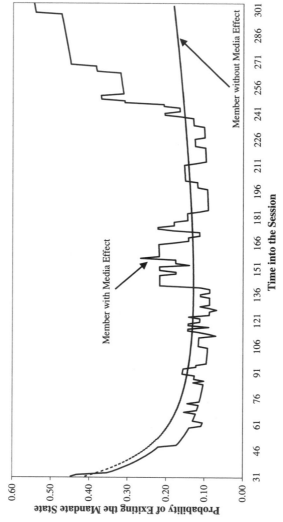

FIGURE 3.13. Hazard Rate of the Mandate, with and without Media Effects.

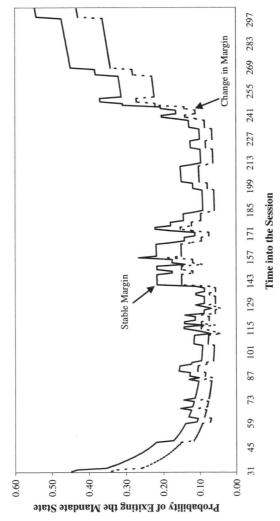

FIGURE 3.14. Hazard Rate of the Mandate by Change in Victory Margin.

predicted hazard rates for a member who gained or lost one standard deviation over the mean change (given the test of equality reported earlier, gains and changes are specified to have equal effects). Members whose victory margin is stable exit more quickly. They receive no direct message from their constituents and, therefore, return to normal more quickly. Change in victory margin induces change in behavior. Across all time points, the member who witnessed a change in victory margin is less likely to exit the mandate state. This movement adds important individual-level confirmation to the mandate thesis; these are precisely the members our theory claims should be most likely to rethink their behavior. We now see that a mandate message is reflected in early roll call votes, and that the strongest carriers of the message are those that our theory predicts should be most responsive.

The final figure (Figure 3.15) presents the strongest of our cross-sectional variables – ideological extremity. As expected, moderates continue to be strongly affected by the mandate, being the least likely to return to their normal voting behavior. The strength of this effect is substantial. Across the days into the session, the difference in the probability of exiting between moderates and extremists ranges from roughly 0.08 to greater than 0.25. Even the smaller differences represent a substantial impact, increasing a member's likelihood of exiting the mandate state by almost 10 percent a day. At its largest effect, it increases the likelihood substantially.

3.6   MEMBERS AND THE MANDATE SIGNAL

When behavior changes following an influential election, a number of stories can explain it. Perhaps the change is due to strategic agenda manipulation by party leaders? Or maybe the early session action is just a few votes on issues raised and settled in the election? These macro-level interpretations are difficult to rule out. However, the individual level evidence we have shown cannot be accounted for by alternative explanations. The patterns in the individual level changes, most notably the effect of the size of the change in the individual member's victory margin, and the dynamic pattern induced by the changing construction of the mandate story can be explained only by the theory of mandate reactions posited here.

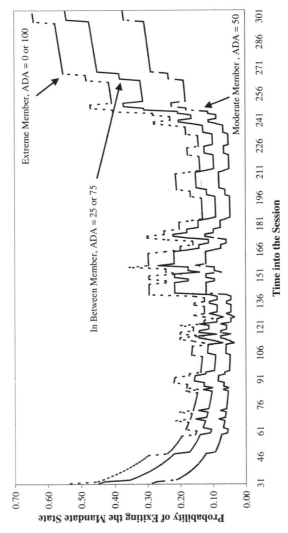

FIGURE 3.15. Hazard Rate of the Mandate by Ideological Extremity.

The patterns across the two questions (who is affected and for how long) are also informative of how mandates influence members of Congress. The answers to these two questions are similar: ideological extremity mitigates the influence of the mandate, whereas being in the mandate party or receiving large losses in the margin of victory augments it. There are also important differences in the patterns. For instance, seniority is unrelated to the likelihood of being affected. Members of Congress are equally likely to respond to the mandate across levels of experience. Given that a member responds, however, more senior members will return to normal more quickly. This suggests that messages about public opinion taken from election results and the postelection interpretation are commonly read to say the same thing. All members, regardless of how many elections they have responded to, can do this. The daily tracking and updating of the state of public opinion, however, appears to be a learned skill. More experienced members do it better. They update their perceptions of public opinion more readily and are affected by the mandate for a much shorter period of time.

The change in the margin of victory results suggests a second important pattern. Individual level signals of change strongly influence members of Congress, and whether the change is good or bad for the member influences how much it matters. Returning to the explanation of who is immediately affected, losses matter, gains do not. Those who see significant losses in their margin of victory initially move toward the mandate in an effort to adjust to the new belief about public opinion. When updating these beliefs, however, gains and losses are equal. The answer to "how long" indicates that if a member is affected, the size, but not the direction, of the change influences how long the changes last. In sum, losses move members in the first place, but all changes are equally strong signals once the session begins.

The results presented so far indicate that individual members of Congress respond to perceptions of a mandate by changing how they vote on policy. It is possible that the sum of individual responses might not translate neatly into an aggregate response that can meaningfully change the final output of congressional policy making. If, for example, only ideologically extreme members changed their votes, then the vote on a policy designed to appeal to the median ideological position within the Congress might not change. Ideologically extreme members are not often pivotal to the formation of a winning coalition. Ideologically moderate members are more often the pivotal votes. It is precisely these members who exhibit the strongest response to the perceived mandate. Thus, we can expect that there would be substantial changes in the outcomes of roll call votes and policy outputs. For these influences, we look to aggregate behavior.

4

The Pattern of Congressional Response

In legislatures, we care about individual votes because we want to understand why members vote as they do. We care about aggregate outcomes because they become public policy. The task of this chapter is to come to terms with the aggregate, to ask how mandates affect which side wins and loses, and how the strength of the winning coalition affects the content of the proposals that become law.

Our opening assumption is that change at the individual level surely heralds some kind of change in aggregate outcomes. But aggregation of individual behaviors into institutional outcomes leaves room for diminution, for exaggeration, and for subtle transformation of the individual impetus in the vote. Thus, we expect to see mandate influences in the institution, having seen them in votes, but it is by no means obvious that they will be the same as what we have already seen.

Our task in this chapter is threefold. First we look at aggregate evidence of voting in Congress to see whether the patterns of individual movement in response to mandate perceptions leave their mark on aggregate voting outcomes. This analysis treats the institution as simply an aggregate of its members. Then we pursue institutional theories for a more sophisticated understanding of how both election results and, independently, their perceived meaning, translate individual into institutional change. And, last, we return to the measures of aggregate change to see if they are responsive to the time-varying signals of the meaning of the previous election.

4.1 CONGRESS IN THE AGGREGATE

The patterns of the previous chapter, early movement toward the mandate followed by later return to normal voting, imply a similar surge and decay in aggregate outcomes. The mandate side of the ideological divide, all things equal, should see heavy majorities early in the session, which eventually decline to the closer divides common in two-party legislatures and consistent with coalition theory (Riker 1962).

The "all things equal" here is a fairly demanding requirement that the content of proposals be comparable. Because no two proposals are exactly comparable, that amounts to the assumption that, given enough votes, comparability will arise from numbers. It is easy to imagine, for example, that a comparison of two votes could go badly astray because one of them was simply easier to agree to and therefore drew larger numbers in support. So to observe the mandate effect in aggregate vote totals we count on putting together strings of hundreds of votes on the assumption that numerous and diverse measures are likely to capture the pattern – even when individual measures would not. With hundreds of votes we simply ignore the content of proposals, array the votes from beginning to end of the session, and expect the mandate side to win with bigger majorities in the beginning than it does regularly or at the end.

To get really big numbers, we put our three mandate sessions and both houses together for one look at voting patterns in mandate years. Votes are those selected by the ideological screen used in Chapter 3 and then reflected so that instead of measuring liberalism or conservatism, they measure the direction of the mandate for the session, liberalism for 1965 and conservatism for 1981 and 1995.[1] To gain statistical power we cumulate so that vote n stands for the average liberalism (or conservatism, depending upon the year) to that point in the session. As a result, we expect to see some variability early in the session, when few votes have contributed to the cumulation, followed by a more steady and predictable response later.[2]

---

[1] In order to get dissimilar data onto a single graph, we have adjusted the cumulative ideology of each house and year to a common norm of fifty and we also have combined different numbers of votes per chamber or year to get approximate equivalence of time. If one house or year had, say, five times as many roll calls as another, then each data point for that house is the average of five votes.

[2] And patterns at the very start are poor evidence for or against the thesis.

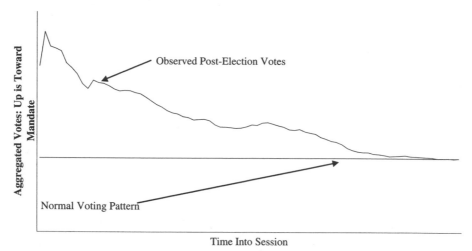

FIGURE 4.1. All Years and Both Houses Combined.

The big aggregation, all ideological votes for both houses for three sessions, is shown in Figure 4.1 Although it covers up patterns across years and chambers that are not so consistent, as we will soon see, the grand aggregation is a stark picture of mandate effects. It shows that the mandate advantaged side wins big early in the session and continues to dominate for half to two-thirds of the session before normal patterns reassert themselves.

Although the transformations applied to the data prevent reading directly the size of winning majorities, it is unusually large majorities on many votes that produce the bulge of Figure 4.1. Does it matter that the mandate position wins by majorities much larger than 50 percent + 1? It does. The essence of legislation, it is often said, is compromise. Those who make proposals would like to see them pass in their strongest form. Proposals to regulate need enforcement with teeth. Proposals for new programs need generous authorizations, billions of dollars for uniform national programs, not mere millions for demonstration grants. Those who propose to cut top income tax rates would prefer not to water down such cuts to cut taxes also for low-income workers. In normal times, compromises are necessary to build a winning majority. The phrase often uttered is, "Half a loaf is better than none." So we do have regulations without adequate enforcement, demonstration grants instead of programs, tax cuts that are not fully targeted on top incomes. That is normal politics.

Extraordinary majorities require no such compromise. They can enact tough legislation, designed to meet its goals and to overcome all obstacles in its path. Because legislative leaders are extraordinarily good vote counters, they can know early in the process whether or not compromise is necessary, and it won't be there if it isn't needed for passage. Thus, what differs between mandate sessions and normal ones is not that proposals pass. They always do. It is that the proposals that pass really make a difference. Sorting through the specifics of what passes and what doesn't is the business of the next chapter. Here we just assert that those big majorities aren't wasted; they produce legislation that, whether for good or ill, really changes things.

Now we unpack our six cases – House and Senate for three mandate years – to look beneath the big pattern already seen. As we lose the advantage of very large numbers of cases, we also will lose the obvious patterns that we have seen in them. In the six cases, we will see five that more or less mimic the grand pattern, one with no pattern at all.

4.1.1 1965

The 1965 House is the aggregate case that shows no mandate effect at all. The net liberalism of the House that year is essentially a (very liberal) constant over the year. (See Figure 4.2.[3]) Although we do not know for sure, we think the 1965 case is a result of an election so decisive in creating a liberal House majority that the usual dynamics of rounding up support wherever it can be found did not occur. Liberals, and the Johnson White House that spearheaded their efforts, did not need any conservative or moderate votes for their program. They had enough support to pass what they wanted and did. Legislation was written in the White House, ratified by party votes in committee virtually unchanged – and with Republican attendance only symbolic – and then easily passed on the floor. In the normal case, nothing of substance can be passed without gathering support from beyond the ranks of an ideological majority. This process guides mandate induced

---

[3] In the three year-specific figures, we graph the roll call cumulations from vote 11 onward because the initial votes are so highly variable as to otherwise visually dominate the graph.

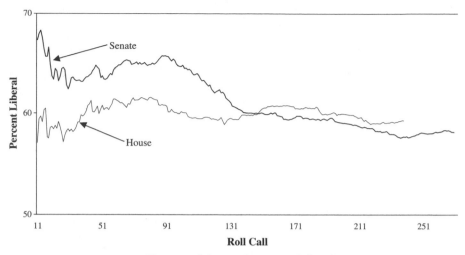

FIGURE 4.2. House and Senate Aggregate Liberalism, 1965.

behavior to add to the winning side. In 1965, that usual coalition building process was absent.

The 89th Senate, in contrast, shows very strong mandate influence. Although the net liberalism of both bodies was similar over the full year, the Senate was much more liberal in the beginning and more conservative at the end. The Senate, with the balance of power controlled by Southern Democrats, was not reliably liberal like the House. The Southerners then – largely for the last time – were deeply conservative, their votes not available at all for anything with racial overtones (and much of the Great Society was closely associated with racial issues). Thus, the Great Society legislation could not pass the Senate without moderate support; some Republicans and Southern Democrats had to be brought on board to win.[4] Under mandate influence early in the session that moderate support was added to the coalition that produced the Great Society. Later in the year – and all through 1966 – that moderate support was no longer available and the tone in Washington changed permanently as a result.

---

[4] Perhaps the reason that liberals in the House did not use their voting power to create even stronger legislation was that such legislation could not pass in the Senate. For this sort of pragmatic consideration, it is important that effective legislative leadership came from the Johnson White House.

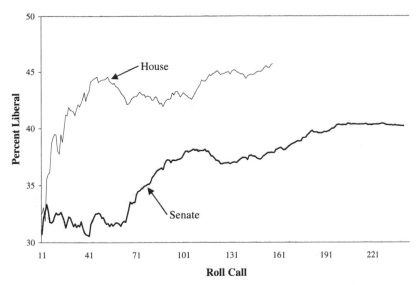

FIGURE 4.3. House and Senate Aggregate Liberalism, 1981.

One of the new faces of national Republican politics in the 1964 loss was Ronald Reagan. He would dominate the face of Republican politics for the next electoral mandate of 1980.

4.1.2 1981

On election night 1980, prospects for legislative success of the new Reagan Administration would not have been bright. Winning a stunning victory over Jimmy Carter, Reagan and his party also took control of the U.S. Senate. But the House, as had always been the case since 1954, belonged to the Democrats. Nothing would happen without the support of members of the defeated party. That Reagan did have his way with Congress, at least for a few months, is history. Something needs to explain why. That something is of course the perception that Ronald Reagan had won a mandate for his proposed conservative policies.

We examine Reagan's Republican Senate and the Democratic House in Figure 4.3 There we see the expected party difference, the Republican controlled Senate uniformly more conservative than the nominally Democratic House. The more important pattern is that both chambers moved toward Reagan's conservative policies in the early months of

1981. Despite its Democratic majority, the House moved well toward the conservative end of the scale in those early months, permitting passage of the omnibus budget resolution in which the whole Reagan package of tax cuts, domestic spending cuts, and defense increases was packaged.

The House could only have become conservative if Democrats were voting for the Reagan proposals. The Senate, in contrast, could have passed the Reagan proposals without the effects of mandate. But mandate effects are nonetheless clearly in evidence, longer lasting, if not as consequential, than those in the House. The Senate moved well to the right of its eventual normal level and stayed there for roughly half of the 1981 session. We know from the analyses of Chapter 3 that those in motion were mainly moderates, conservative Democrats and liberal Republicans. Both were threatened by the mandate perception. Democrats faced the prospect of defeat at the hands of Republican opponents in general elections. Liberal Republicans had reason to fear conservative opponents in their own party's primaries. Both changed their voting patterns until eventually returning to normal on reassessment that the mandate story was overblown.

4.1.3   1995

The politics of 1994 were dominated by the failed Clinton healthcare reform, which wasn't much talked about by election time, and by the "Contract with America," which was. To nationalize the campaign Newt Gingrich and the Republican House leadership put together a package of ten legislative items that had the property that they were both part of the conservative agenda and also known (by focus group studies) to play well with the public. To publicize the Contract the Republican leadership bought a full page ad in *The Reader's Digest* and then referred to the ad in frequent media appearances thereafter. The Contract idea proved to be popular and most Republican House candidates campaigned on it. Democrats, sensing the public appeal of the Contract, decided to run against it, with many changing prepositions, branding it the "Contract *on* America."

Election night settled the issue decisively in the Republican's favor. The huge gain of House seats, and along with it majority control, naturally elevated the Contract to mandate status. Seizing on historical

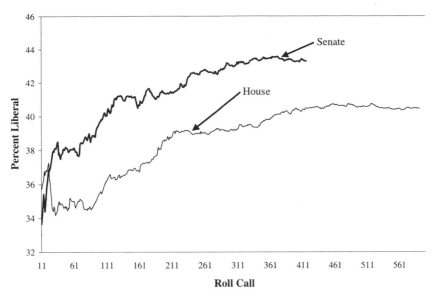

FIGURE 4.4. House and Senate Aggregate Liberalism, 1995.

analogy, Newt Gingrich went further, claiming that the Contract was a revolutionary change of direction, and promising to pass all its ten items in the "first one hundred days" of the 104th Congress. By the time the new Congress was seated, the genuinely impressive Republican victory had become a revolution, with a spotlight on the House of Representatives as center of American government – as never before or since. The small Republican majority, with the help of frightened Democrats, spent the first one hundred days acting with uniform purpose, attaining a level of conservatism well beyond the election result (see Figure 4.4). After calling it the Contract *on* America, most of the Democrats who had campaigned against it found two or three of the Contract items for which they could vote.

The Contract, it is important to recall, was a *House* Republican program, never coordinated with the national party or the Senate campaign. Republican Senate candidates were spectators to the Contract campaign, almost as much so as Democrats. If the mandate of 1994 were only for the specifics of the Contract, then there was no mandate in the Senate. The Senate response in Figure 4.4 tells us something important. At least as large as for the House, the U.S. Senate response was to move dramatically to the right of its normal position, more liberal than the House (but still pretty conservative). This is consistent with an interpretation that Senators of both parties took the 1994 election to signal generalized conservatism, not merely support for the ten popular Contract items. Indeed, the Contract itself did not fare well in the Republican Senate.

We have now looked at individuals and at aggregates, seeing the same pattern in both. Lawmaking, however, does not proceed by simple aggregation. The structure of American political institutions conditions how inputs are translated into outputs – or often fail to be. We need, accordingly, to deal with some of the complexity of institutions, to ascertain whether constitutional requirements and legislative rules dampen or enhance the mandate impulse.

4.2   PIVOTAL POLITICS

Our vehicle for dealing with institutional complexity is Krehbiel's (1998) excellent theory of "pivotal politics." Krehbiel asks how we can explain that simple majorities sometimes prevail in legislatures, but often do not. His answer is that the process of lawmaking in the United States encounters multiple pivots, key points at which the preferences of individual actors block or allow the flow of legislation.

Duncan Black's (1958) early insight about the median voter is in many ways the beginning of formal understanding of institutions. Black observes that the outcomes of a legislature with a single dimension issue space (and single-peaked preferences) depend predominantly on the preferences of a key pivotal member, the median of the left to right lineup. Given a proposal from either ideological wing, if the median member prefers the proposal to the status quo, then a winning coalition can be constructed, which includes that one member and all others to the left or right, depending on the proposal. The insight that follows is that agenda setters, let us say from the left of the spectrum, must craft legislation that is just moderate enough to win the support of the median member. Doing less would not result in a win. Going further would be making unnecessary concessions.

The median voter theorem holds for hypothetical committees or legislatures that act under simple majority rule, unimpeded by external constraints or internal procedures. Lawmaking in the United States is a more complicated matter. Constitutional requirements that legislation pass both houses of Congress in identical form and then receive a presidential signature (with some variations and exceptions) erect a further set of barriers. And one of the two houses, the Senate, under Rule 22, allows 40 percent + 1 of the members to block the outcome of a majority decision by filibuster. Thus, to become law, a bill must attain simple majorities in both houses, surmount a possible filibuster in the Senate, gain a presidential signature or, failing that, put together a two-thirds majority in both houses to override the veto.

Here we review the central features of the pivotal politics theory and then apply it to clarify mandate institutional dynamics.

4.2.1 Notes on Pivotal Politics Theory

The theory is a four-stage game in which players have rational expectations over future stages at each round of play – that is, they anticipate later stages, for example, the likelihood of a Senate filibuster, and shape proposals in order to prevail in the whole game, not merely the stage. Define:

Symbol	Pivot
p	the president's ideal point
q	the status quo
m	the ideal point of the median player
f	the ideal point of the filibuster pivot
v	the ideal point of the veto pivot. The veto pivot is defined relative to p, the president's position.

In stage 1, a proposal is made by m that will be preferred to the status quo, q, by m and all members to his or her left or right. Then, in stage 2, opponents in the Senate choose whether or not to filibuster the proposal. The pivotal actor here is the filibuster pivot, f, the sixtieth member to join an ideological coalition from left or right. If f prefers the proposal to q, a filibuster will not succeed and the legislation will be passed. If not, then opponents can potentially block the legislation or cause it to be modified so that it can win the support of f.

In stage 3, the president decides whether or not to veto legislation not to his liking. His key consideration is whether the veto will be sustained or overridden. That requires anticipation of stage 4, in which

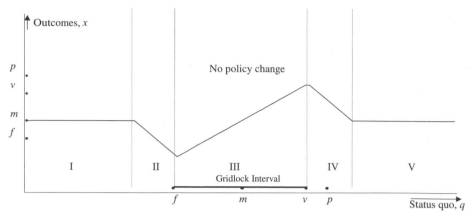

FIGURE 4.5. Krehbiel's "Equilibrium policies in the pivotal politics theory." (Source: Krehbiel 1998, Figure 2.7, p. 35.)

the pivotal actor is the veto pivot, that member from the side supporting the legislation who can add his or her vote to opponents and go beyond the two-thirds necessary to override the presidential veto.

The model produces outcomes in five "zones" from left to right. (See Figure 4.5.) If the status quo, q, lies outside the range defined by the filibuster and veto pivots – zones I and V – then the simple majority preference, m, acquires supermajority support and becomes law. This, in Krehbiel's terms, is full convergence, an unlikely outcome because it requires that previous policy makers (using the same rules) chose a q that was unpopular. Thus, the policy dominance of the median member, the essence of the median voter theorem of Black (1958), is also unlikely.

In the partial convergence zones – II on the left and IV on the right – m's preferred position draws majority support but can be blocked by other pivots. That entails that the proposal must be changed, watered down, to expand the majority from a simple majority to one large enough to include the potential blocking pivot. Thus, legislation may pass, but it will not be in the strong version that would have commanded majority support. It is the "half a loaf," which is such a familiar outcome of legislative activity.

Zone III in the middle, between the veto and filibuster pivots, produces "gridlock," the definition of which is that proposals for change to the status quo that could have commanded majority support do not

TABLE 4.1. *Pivot Positions Before and After the 1964 Election, Liberalism Propensities*

Pivot	Symbol	1964 (Before)	1965 (After)
Median	*m*	0.642	0.707
Filibuster	*f*	0.544	0.531
Veto	*v*	0.867	0.888
President	*p*	0.662	0.629

become law.[5] This is nonconvergence, a state of affairs in which there is much wheel spinning and appearance of action but no outcome.

We are now ready to think about how mandates interact with pivotal politics. We do so in two stages, first looking at pure election effects, how the personnel of government after the election are different from those before. Then we look at dynamics, how the same people change over the session under the influence of the mandate message.

4.2.2 Static Effects: Changing Personnel

One way to observe the pure effects of an election is through the change in pivots, before and after. Using the same individual liberalism propensities as before we observe median, filibuster, veto, and president both before and after.

1964 and the 89th Congress. Begin with the 88th Congress. From Table 4.1, the "before" column, we can see what we know from history, the 88th Congress was already very liberal before the election sweep of 1964 made the 89th even more so. The Congress that produced the Civil Rights Act of 1964 and more of the Kennedy/Johnson liberal agenda than any of its predecessors had a median member, at about 64 percent liberal, well into the liberal range.[6] Even the more conservative filibuster pivot is on the liberal end of the scale.[7] This Congress should have produced liberal legislation.

---

[5] Our usage of "gridlock," like Krehbiel's original, is of this formal definition, frustrated potential majorities, and not the more colorful connotations of popular usage.

[6] The median and veto pivots are averages of House and Senate medians and pivots, while the filibuster of course is purely a Senate phenomenon.

[7] For consistency we use the 60th senator from the left as the filibuster estimate, but the actual rule until 1975 was two-thirds of those present and voting.

To understand the ideological impact of the 1964 sweep we must take account of a party system then quite different from what it is now. Then the alignment of ideology with region was much stronger than it is now and the alignment of ideology with party was weaker. As a result, many of the Democratic congressional wins had no impact on the median pivot. They were contests in which both parties fielded candidates from the same end of the spectrum, liberals in the North, conservatives in the South. The GOP gains in the deep South, for example, came entirely at the expense of very conservative Democrats. Those exchanges have no influence in the pivotal politics theory, which has no role for party numbers or party control issues.

Thus, we see movement toward liberalism in the median pivot to about 71 percent liberal, but not as large as might have been expected from a big party win. The filibuster pivot is essentially unchanged, consistent with the small Senate turnover of the 1964 election. And the veto pivot, very liberal already, also is little changed from the 88th. The presidency measure, which reflects the views of members of the two houses who regularly support the president's position, probably understates Lyndon Johnson's true liberalism. The slight decline from 1964 to 1965 doesn't mean that Johnson become more conservative, but that he expanded his support base beyond the ranks of the most liberal members – and conservative was the only possible direction for expansion.

The "Fabulous 89th Congress" was in position to pass liberal legislation. But there was still no guarantee. The gridlock interval in pivotal theory was small – the distance between Lyndon Johnson (sixty-three) and the sixty-first senator in a liberal coalition to defeat a filibuster (fifty-four) was small, but not zero. And if LBJ was to propose radical changes to public policy – and he was – that nonzero interval should have blocked some proportion of those proposals from becoming law.

1980 and the 97th Congress. The 1964 election, sweep though it was, left the same president in office dealing with the both houses of Congress in the unchanged control of his own party. The Reagan 1980 victory, in contrast, changed the presidency and party control in the U.S. Senate. Thus, we expect more dramatic changes in the pivots, and with dramatic consequences. Before the election, a liberal president

TABLE 4.2. *Pivot Positions Before and After the 1980 Election, Liberalism Propensities*

Pivot	Symbol	1980 (Before)	1981 (After)
Median	m	0.628	0.378
Filibuster	f	0.564	0.489
Veto	v	0.828	0.185
President	p	0.588	0.189

(59 percent) faced a liberal median voter (63 percent) in both houses and even a liberal filibuster pivot (56 percent; see Table 4.2). The election changed everything. The median member was now on the conservative end of the scale (38 percent) and proposals from that median position could bypass filibuster without requiring the votes of any liberals. The president's position of course switched from the liberal end of the scale to a very conservative 19 percent. The big change in the veto pivot is a reflection of the presidential change; a conservative president needs one-third support to sustain a veto and that naturally comes first from his own end of the ideological spectrum.

The theory of pivotal politics would predict limited legislative success for the Reagan program, an accurate prediction for the 97th Congress as a whole, if not for its first months. The gridlock interval, the space between the president's position (nineteen) and the filibuster pivot (forty-nine), is very large. Proposals in that range should achieve simple majorities but fail to pass in the face of the filibuster threat. Reagan's early success thus becomes an anomaly.[8]

1994 and the 104th Congress. Before the 1994 election a liberal president and a liberal median member of Congress demonstrated that uniform party control is no panacea for legislative action. Bill

---

[8] Krehbiel adds a wrinkle that predicts the appearance of presidential honeymoons in legislative success. The idea is that new presidents inherit the status quo of their predecessors, which are equilibrium outcomes of the previous regime, not the current one. Those policies, out of line with current congressional preferences, then become easy to defeat. Once passed, the new status quo, in line with current preferences, then induces gridlock going forward; the early success explains later inaction. The argument is entirely about congressional preferences, having no link to any status of the president except newness. Honeymoons of presidential success in this argument are not honeymoons and not presidential.

TABLE 4.3. *Pivot Positions Before and After the 1994 Election, Liberalism Propensities*

Pivot	Symbol	1994 (Before)	1995 (After)
Median	m	0.723	0.258
Filibuster	f	0.509	0.674
Veto	v	0.832	0.743
President	p	0.728	0.960

Clinton's fellow Democrats gave him some small victories, for example, the 1993 tax increase, and one very big defeat, the administration's number one priority national healthcare program. The 1994 election changed things so drastically that presidential proposals became pro forma. The congressional median changed overnight from very liberal (72 percent) to very conservative (26 percent; see Table 4.3). The filibuster pivot becomes more liberal, not because Congress was, but because it was now conservative proposals that would lead to liberal filibusters, the reverse of the preelection situation. With a very conservative median member confronting liberal filibuster and veto pivots, the 104th was designed for legislative stalemate. No surprise then that the 104th Congress passed legislation that did not become law, in effect most of the Contract with America, and became known principally for an act of gridlock in its purest form, shutting down the government over a budgetary deadlock.

One of the strengths of the pivotal politics theory is that it highlights the changes of pivotal players between one regime and the next. The veto pivot, for example, is not particularly crucial for a president dealing with a like-minded Congress, for example, Bill Clinton in 1994. It becomes crucial with the outcome of the 1994 election producing majority proposals that the president opposes. Then the key leverage of the presidency is the ability to summon one-third of either house to sustain the president's veto – or more often, threat of veto.

We have exploited the estimation of pivot positions from election results to capture the pure effect of personnel changes. These are entirely free of mandate effects. The virtue of the approach is that we can now estimate dynamics over the postelection Congress to observe pure mandate effects.

4.2.3   Dynamic Effects: Changing the Message

In pivotal politics terms, a mandate may be expressed as a unit of pure information, the consequence of which is that members reevaluate q, the policy status quo, as undesirable. A "mandate for change" is a voter command to not leave the status quo untouched. If q becomes undesirable, then alternatives such as m, the position of the median member, gain in relative desirability. Thus, even with no change in membership there is room for changed outcomes of the legislative process. As m becomes more preferred to q, then it becomes more likely to acquire the supermajority necessary to become law.

In normal politics, the comparison of m to q is symmetrical. A change that goes too far is politically dangerous just as is a reversion to the status quo. Under the force of a mandate, that symmetry vanishes. If members think voters have commanded "no q," then any alternative that can be labeled "reform" becomes more desirable. In this situation successful legislation, passing something, becomes politically preferred to inaction and the normal inclination to block change is replaced by a desire to go on record as having favored "reform," that is, changing q.

We now have static q, the policy status quo of the new Congress, and all the pivots, fixed by the election. We define the consensus on mandate to mean that voters have sent a message rejecting q. All the comparisons, for example, m to q, are affected by belief in the message. If there is a mandate, then q is less desirable to all actors than previously believed. But q is an unobserved term in pivotal theory. What we can observe is how often proposals to change the status quo pass and how much support they draw. If, in the case of 1965, for example, the conservative status quo from the Eisenhower years is particularly unacceptable early in 1965, then we should observe movements toward liberalism of all the pivots at that time, which then decay back toward the norm as the message is progressively discounted by new information flow over the session.

89th Congress. We can estimate the moving positions of each of the pivots as a session of Congress proceeds. We do that for the 89th Congress in Figure 4.6. We can imagine a scenario in which the distribution of ideologies is so skewed that aggregate movements do not

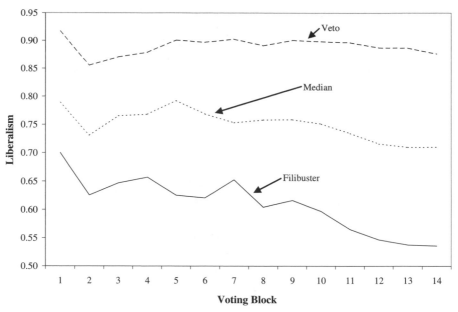

FIGURE 4.6. Dynamic Pivots in the 89th Congress.

entail similar movement for each of the pivots. The message of that figure and two more to come is to the contrary. What we see in pivot movements over the term is pretty much what we would have expected from earlier analyses.

Movements of the median and veto pivots in the 89th Congress are an average of the nonmoving House and fairly substantial movements in the Senate. What we see in the figure then is small movement, showing the characteristic mandate dynamic. The effect is uniform; a more liberal median member in the Krehbiel theory proposes more liberal legislation, which then passes because the pivots that might block the legislation are themselves more liberal than normal.

97th Congress. The new Reagan Congress of 1981 in Figure 4.7 shows far more dramatic movements. With House and Senate medians deeply in conservative territory and the filibuster still safely conservative, the early Reagan Administration could propose dramatic changes in public policy and have them pass. We earlier noted that Reagan's early legislative success was something of an anomaly, that the members elected in November 1980 were not conservative enough to pass that

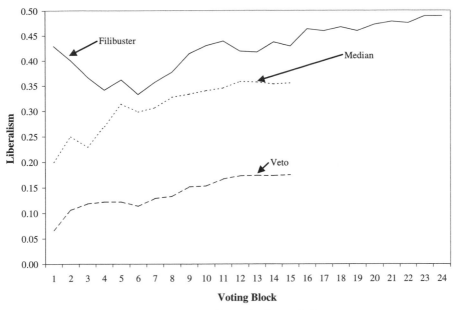

FIGURE 4.7. Dynamic Pivots in the 97th Congress.

program – particularly with Democratic control of the House. Here there is no anomaly. The program could pass because this Congress was very much more conservative in the spring, when the key proposals were debated and passed, then it would be later on.

104th Congress. To understand the movement of pivots for the 104th Congress in Figure 4.8 we must first understand party polarization at the time. The earlier cases show movement across the ideological scale with moderates particularly sensitive to the mandate message. It is an overstatement to say that the 104th Congress had no moderates, but only by a little. By 1995, most Democrats had moved to the left end of the scale, consistently supporting the liberal party position, and most Republicans had done the opposite. Combined with a near 50–50 party division that meant that neither the conservative Congress nor the liberal president was close to all of the pivots. Going beyond a simple majority in the 104th meant acquiring support from the other party. With both parties clustered near the extremes, that made supermajorities unusually difficult.

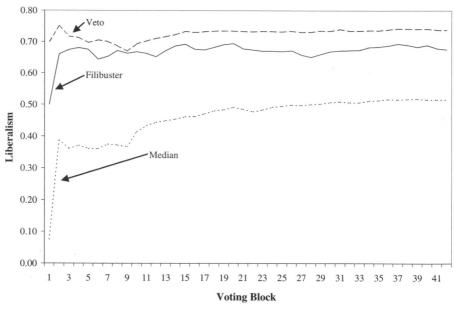

FIGURE 4.8. Dynamic Pivots in the 104th Congress.

The median voter in 1995 was in both houses a Republican, but just barely. The filibuster pivot in the Senate was a Democrat at a time when even the most conservative Democrats were considerably more liberal than Republicans. And the veto pivot for the Democratic president was a quite liberal Democrat. This then is the classic gridlock formula. The preferences of simple majorities could be and were blocked by procedural barriers that required more than simple majorities. The very impressive head of steam for the Contract with America package produced many winning votes, particularly in the House. It didn't produce much law, because almost none of it could overcome the filibuster threat in the Senate or override a presidential veto. Here the pivotal theory is really illuminating, showing why a quite determined majority could not legislate.

4.3 MOVEMENT BACK TOWARD EQUILIBRIUM: A LONGER VIEW

We have now seen much evidence that members, individually and in the aggregate, deviate from equilibrium voting following the mandate election and then return to it later. Our task here is to take a longer view of this process, to see if our theory can help explain why and at what rate the return to equilibrium occurs.

This is not a new question that we address here. The duration analyses of the previous chapter address fundamentally the same issues. Here we dispense with the complexities of hazard functions – the necessary apparatus of individual-level analysis – and look at the simpler issues of aggregate movement over time. Our theory is that members respond to the shock of unexpected election sweeps with behavioral change, which then decays as the election recedes into the past and as commentary in the Washington community gradually reassesses the mandate.[9]

We can observe movement over time in aggregate voting patterns, the data of Figures 4.3 and 4.4.[10] We already know that a pattern of impulse and decay back to equilibrium will be found. We ask here whether that is all there is, whether responses are just temporary from the simple passage of time – novelty, after all, always wears off – or whether information flows of two kinds play a role in the process. Our most direct indicator of information is media commentary, which we take as a proxy for the buzz about public opinion of the congressional cloakrooms. And we will look, too, to a less direct indicator, public response to two presidents, Ronald Reagan who embodied the mandate message of 1981 and Bill Clinton who opposed the Republican revolution of 1995.

4.3.1 Measures

The voting blocks of Chapter 3 and of Figures 4.1 to 4.4 are not uniform in time. Some ten-vote blocks last a month or more,[11] some just three or four days. For the analysis to come, we require something more regular. Monthly aggregation produces regular behavior in our

---

[9] We do not rule out a mandate claim that may withstand time and experience to become permanent, in which case no equilibration is expected. But our half century view of American politics yields only temporary cases.

[10] We will not address the 1965 case for lack of adequate media commentary data.

[11] Recall that the blocks are ten consecutive *ideological* votes. Counting the nonideological roll calls with which they are intermixed, the sequence of roll calls may be as long as twenty-five or thirty.

various measures but too few cases for analysis. Looking at daily intervals provides plenty of cases, but our media measures do not exist
on most days of the year and about half also have no roll call votes in
Congress. We settle on a unit in between: weeks.

To see the regular evolution of behavior amid all the to and fro
of normal politics we cumulate the measures of media commentary
and of voting to capture the big picture of response over the year.
That decision gives our resulting time series integrated properties that
threaten spurious associations if used with ordinary regressions. We
employ an error correction formulation to deal with that statistical
issue.

We begin with a visual look at the patterns of movement in
Figure 4.9, which displays for 1981 cumulative voting in the direction of the mandate for House and Senate, the net balance of media
commentary that claims that the 1980 election expressed a mandate
for conservatism (percent pro over total number of stories) and the
approval ratings of Ronald Reagan. Time, on the horizontal axis, is
the sixty-one-week span between election week 1980 and the end of
calendar year 1981.

The key measures of Figure 4.9, the consensus of commentary and
the House and Senate response after the new Congress begins, quite
clearly run together. The pattern of member voting is much the same as

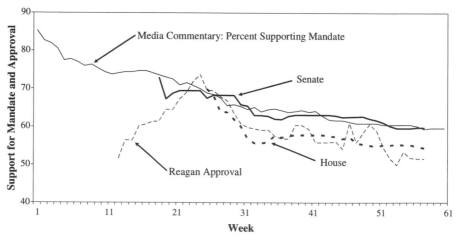

FIGURE 4.9. Evolving Support for the Mandate in 1981: Media Commentary,
House and Senate Mandate Voting, and Reagan Approval Ratings.

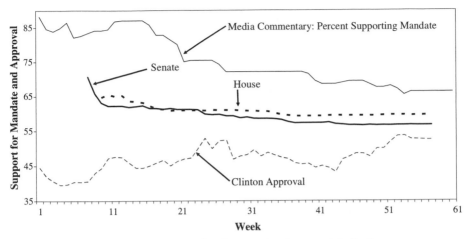

FIGURE 4.10. Evolving Support for the Mandate in 1995: Media Commentary, House and Senate Mandate Voting, and Clinton Approval Ratings.

the public interpretation, moving away from initial shock and toward eventual equilibration together. Ronald Reagan, the key actor who gave his name to the mandate, would be expected to draw public approval and disapproval in some proportion to the public belief in mandate. And like the media commentary on the election, approval of President Reagan would signal to Congress that the public supported movement toward Reagan's conservative views. But approval is less regular than the other series for two reasons. It is not cumulated over time and we also know that approval is strongly responsive to economic performance, which is unrelated to the mandate signal. The early months of 1981 produced good economic news, in dramatic contrast to the previous year. And then Reagan's numbers spiked from his survival and good-humored response to an attempted assassination in April.

We observe the same four weekly aggregations for the 1994–1995 case in Figure 4.10. Here the media commentary and House and Senate voting series show the same parallelism as in the earlier 1981 case. But the role of the president is more complicated and less apparently part of the story. Bill Clinton was the official villain of the 1994 Republican revolution. So we would expect his approval to run counter to media commentary and to mandate voting in Congress. An approved Bill Clinton would be information that the electorate had second thoughts about its November votes. And the figure shows some of that in the late weeks of 1995 as Congress and the president prepared for what was to become an historic showdown over the federal budget. But aside from that modest movement, it is hard to see much that is regular or predictable about the 1995 public response to the Clinton presidency.

To capture the patterns of association in these data requires more than the eyes can see. Causality in time series is a subtle matter. It requires statistical modeling, to which we now turn.

4.3.2 Modeling Equilibration

Our micro model of the member response, reaction to the news of mandate followed by gradual return to normal voting patterns, predicts equilibration in the aggregate. An equilibrating time series is one that responds to shocks – also called errors – and then tends to "correct" itself, returning to normal. This is precisely what is captured in an error correction model.

The error correction formulation models a dependent series as existing in an equilibrium relationship with causal variables, encountering shocks ("errors") that move it away from equilibrium and then correcting those shocks. It captures two conceptually distinct kinds of causality, the correction process that occurs because the variables are in an equilibrium relationship with one another, and the short-term movement of a change in the dependent series as a direct response to a change in the independent series. Accordingly, two kinds of inference are relevant to the issue of cause. One is evidence of correction, seen in the (negative) coefficient on the lagged value of the dependent series when predicting the first difference, Δy, of y. This, in conjunction with a significant association between the lagged level of an independent variable, leads to the inference of equilibrium seeking causality. The second is the short-term flow from the first difference of explanatory variables to the first difference of the dependent series. It is uncommon for both types to be present and either is sufficient for inference of causality.

We observe the evidence for both years in Table 4.4. For this analysis, we combine House and Senate voting into a single series for each year. It is an average of the two when both are present and the Senate series for a few weeks in which Senate votes are available and House votes are not.

TABLE 4.4. *Aggregate Voting Outcomes over the Term Explained by Media Commentary and Presidential Approval (Error Correction), 1981 and 1995*

Variables	1981	1995
Lagged Mandate Voting (Error Correction)	-0.55^a	-0.46^a
	(0.11)	(0.04)
Media Commentary		
First Difference	-0.17	0.09^a
	(0.25)	(0.045)
Lagged Level	0.28^a	0.12^a
	(0.10)	(0.01)
Presidential Approval		
First Difference	0.14^a	0.04
	(0.07)	(0.03)
Lagged Level	0.18^a	0.06^a
	(0.05)	(0.02)
Intercept	4.98	15.49
	(2.65)	(1.92)
R^2	.48	.83
N	39	50

Note: Standard errors are in parentheses.
[a] $p < .05$.

Beginning in the "1981" column, we see very strong evidence of error correction. The coefficient on the correction process, -0.55, which is highly significant, tells us that any tendency for congressional votes to deviate from the path of media commentary and Reagan approval (or equally, the reverse) is immediately corrected, with 55 percent of the deviation cast off in the first week and the remainder quickly thereafter. Because the congressional votes respond to the lagged levels of both media commentary (0.28) and Reagan approval (0.18) the case for equilibration is complete. We see an absence of direct causality in the nonsignificant (and incorrectly signed) coefficient on the first difference of commentary and a weak positive case for presidential approval in the significant coefficient (0.14) on approval first differences. Because error correction models predict the first differences of the dependent series – Δy, not y – strong model fit is unusual. Here the explained variance (R^2) of .48 is impressive.

The 1995 case is similar, but with complicating wrinkles. The fit is even better and the error correction rate (-0.46) almost as large (and highly significant). But the equilibrating relationship with media commentary is smaller (0.12), although again very highly significant. And there is a weak (0.09) but significant direct flow from change in media commentary to change in voting. The complex wrinkle here is that the equilibrating relationship with Clinton approval, which should be negative, is instead positive, although quite weak at 0.06. This implies that mandate voting becomes ever so slightly stronger – more conservative – as Clinton becomes more approved, which isn't a sensible relationship. We conclude that this is a statistical fluke, but one that undermines our belief that presidential approval captures some portion of support for or opposition to the mandate interpretation. The Reagan case behaved as theory predicted. The Clinton one did not. We are left not knowing.

What do we know, however, is this: the return to equilibrium is more than the mere passage of time from the original impetus of the preceding election. It actively responds to signals of changing interpretation in the Washington environment.

This closes our case for the congressional response, now clearly seen in both individual and aggregate behaviors. We turn now in Chapter 5 to raising the question of consequences. Does it matter that Congress responds to perceived mandates?

5

Consequences

We wrote in Chapter 1 of great legislative struggles and momentous attempts to compromise them. In this chapter, we return to the issue of the consequences that ensue when the Washington community reaches the consensus that an election carried a message of voter intent. Our job here is to look systematically at the product of mandated Congresses – the laws enacted and policies forever changed – asking first how different was their outcome because of the mandate signal and then how different is public policy in America because these three particular episodes occurred.

We will observe these three Congresses as historical events and then we will take up the more systematic tools of political science to assesses exactly which actions would have been otherwise if not for the mandate signal at the crucial moment of decision. We deal in order with mandate induced changes in rules and procedures, then in a counterfactual analysis of what outcomes might have been without the mandate message, and then we examine the product of these Congresses in the longer view of American public policy.

Before the course of American politics can be altered, Congress must organize itself. Before the policy battles, bill introductions, and roll calls comes the rules. So that is where we begin.

5.1 INSTITUTIONAL POLITICS

Institutions are defined by their rules. The two are inseparable. Rules structure the interactions and incentives of actors, and they define and

limit the set of choices available to individuals (North 1990). Nowhere
is this more true than in legislatures, where organization and procedure
shape the behavior of actors and define legislative strategy. In legislatures, rules are among the most important tools actors use to further
their interests. Understanding the rules is fundamental to understanding the politics of the institution (Schickler 2001).

Existing theories of institutional change suggest that a mandated
Congress is apt to see significant rule changes directed at controlling the
agenda. Theories that emphasize majority party control (Cox and Mc-
Cubbins 1993, 1994), the power of the median voter (Krehbiel 1998;
Schickler 2000), conditional party government (Aldrich and Rhode
2000; Binder 1996, 1997), or multiple competing interests (Schickler
2001) all provide reasons for mandates to prompt efforts at institutional change.

Following a mandate election the median member of Congress
changes from membership replacement and from the mandate induced
changes documented in the two previous chapters. These changes are
most prominent at the outset of a Congress when organization and
procedure are the first acts of governance.

5.1.1   Why Change Rules?

Legislatures, when they organize themselves to do business, face an
always unresolved tension between two impulses. The first of these,
majoritarianism, is the impulse to organize in such a way that a majority can effectively work its will. Rules that expedite simple majority
control come with a cost, however. The power given to majorities to
act is necessarily taken away from somebody. That somebody is the
members themselves as individuals. Rules that permit simple majority
action deprive the members of the power and prerogative that make
legislative life satisfying. The individual impulse organizes legislatures
to make legislative life satisfying for members. The individual influence it creates comes usually at the expense of majority action. When
members have prerogatives, majorities often find themselves unable
to act.

When majorities cannot act the institution and its members are
threatened with loss of collective influence. And the members' individual influence always depends upon collective influence. But rules that

empower majorities also threaten to make ciphers of the members, to make them nothing but their votes. And in eras of party government, their votes are pretty much predetermined. Thus, the tension is never resolved. The balance drifts this way and that, needing correction at fairly frequent intervals. When the pure procedure of the rules becomes enmeshed with context, strategy, and leadership, the balance moves away from center and the impulse for reform is created.

The electoral mandate is likely to provide a spark for procedural reform. With the mandate comes a new urgency to act, to satisfy a restive public. This will create pressure for majoritarian reforms, to create rules that eliminate barriers to action. Under the heat of the mandate signal individual prerogatives give way to the urgent need for quick and forceful action. Moreover, strategic party leaders recognize that the power derived from the mandate can only wane during the session. Thus, they seek rules that will codify the current understanding of politics. These rules seek to tie the hands of legislators later in the session as they reevaluate the meaning of the election and the state of public opinion. The rank and file are likely to follow along with these votes. They cannot afford to oppose these rule changes if the mandate does not wane. For both the leaders and the rank and file, then, the mandate creates clear incentives to change the rules to institutionalize the mandate. Whatever the balance between individual and majority impulses at the moment of mandate then, we expect action to move it in the majoritarian direction.[1]

Mandates also put in place a unique combination of the collective interests Schickler (2001) identified as motivations for changing legislative institutions – member reelection, institutional capacity and prestige, member power within the institution, party interests, and policy interests. The mandate realigns member interests, associating their reelection interest with the policy preferences believed to underlie the electorate's policy signal. The interest to pass the policy outputs associated with the mandate is likely to be dominant. The confluence of interests increases the likelihood of seeing the passage of what Schickler calls a "common carrier," or a single vehicle to satisfy the combined

---

[1] That in turn should create a later dynamic restoring member prerogatives. As the excesses of mandate rules push the balance off center, pressure to recreate member prerogatives should assert itself in the years after the force of the mandate is spent.

interests. In these cases, rule changes would be directed at supporting the power of the mandate party and the mandate agenda.

So we have reason to expect efforts to enact more than nominal change in rules, particularly in the House.[2] But do these expectations hold? What transpired in the first days of these unique Congresses that may have altered the institution and the policy outputs that followed? And were these years unique in these respects? To answer these questions, we begin with a picture of how the three years began. We offer a description of the changes, how they came about, and how they represent unusual politics. We then return to the question of how these changes compare to nonmandate years.

5.1.2 1965: Rules for a Great Society

In approaching the coming session of Congress, President Johnson sought to cultivate the notion that his mandate was "for prudence and restraint, as well as for action and progress (*New York Times*, Jan. 3, 1965, p. E3). He repeatedly mentioned that he would not rush a series of dramatic proposals immediately to Congress and instead would put forth a steady stream of progressive policy changes. The *New York Times* ascribed these motives to the president's desire to "avoid a frontal attack" on Congress and to "to think in terms of four years in office – not just 1964" (*New York Times*, Jan. 3, 1965, p. E3).

The landslide victory was an opportunity for major policy change and, after decades on the sideline without influence, the liberal Democrats were unwilling to waste it.[3] To capitalize on the mandate and their majorities in Congress, the Democrats abandoned normal politics before Congress convened. The mandate and the expanded majorities offered an opportunity to pursue both a new sense of party unity and a set of institutional changes to ease the passage of the president's agenda.

The majorities offered a strong institutional base for the mandate, but the Democrats still faced hurdles to their success. One thing that

---

[2] The Senate is a continuing body. It does not require "organization" at the beginning of a new Congress and thus does not present the same opportunity for rules change on opening day as does the House.

[3] For an unsurpassed treatment of the legislative wilderness of liberalism in the decades before 1964, see Caro (2002).

observers believed the mandate did not do was to "fill in the deep ideological split among the Democrats in Congress" (*New York Times*, Jan.
10, 1965, p. E13). Conservative Southern Democrats posed a significant challenge to the passage of the Great Society. The ideological split
and the threat of disunity had the potential to disrupt liberal Democratic efforts.

A second hurdle would be the procedural rules that opponents of
policy change could use to slow the progress of a bill. Deft use of seem-
ingly innocuous rules could significantly delay bills, if not kill them
outright. Given the transient nature of the mandate effect, the strategy of procedural delay would have strong appeal during periods of
mandate politics.

But how should the mandate party avoid such hurdles? One
means would be to continue to rely on the moderate and liberal
Republicans who had helped pass elements of President Kennedy's
agenda in the previous Congress. With the aid of the 1964 mandate, Democrats could expect some Republican votes in support
of their positions. But the Democrats did not rely solely on partisan crossovers to pass their program. They took action to keep
Democrats in line, to reduce procedural hurdles, and to strengthen the
Democratic leadership, which strongly supported the administration's
policies.

On January 2, the Democratic caucus took the dramatic step of
stripping the seniority of two Southern Democrats who had openly
supported Republican Barry Goldwater during the presidential election. Representatives Albert Watson of South Carolina and John Bell
Williams of Mississippi had both unapologetically supported Goldwater. Before stripped of his seniority, Representative Williams served
eighteen years in the House and was the second-ranking Democrat on
the Interstate and Foreign Commerce Committee, first in line to assume
the chair. The disciplinary act was a stunning signal because it was the
first time in history that a House Democrat had been disciplined for
disloyalty, and the first disciplinary act for any reason since 1911, a
dramatic signal to help maintain unity (*New York Times*, Jan. 3, 1965,
emphasis ours).

The Democratic efforts went further. On the opening day of the session the Democratic leadership passed three rule changes that ensured
swift consideration of proposals and that "saw a significant increase

in the powers of the speaker for the first time this century" (*New York Times*, Jan. 5, 1965, p. 1).

The first change allowed the Speaker to bypass the Rules Committee after a bill had been under its review for twenty-one days. The new rule gave the Speaker discretionary authority to recognize a chair or ranking committee member who could then offer a motion to have a bill placed before the House for consideration on majority approval. This provision made it exceedingly difficult for the Rules Committee, chaired by conservative Representative Howard Smith of Virginia, to obstruct legislation. A second change gave similar powers to the Speaker to call up motions to send bills to conference committees. The change meant that at any time the Speaker could move a bill to conference with simple majority support. Previously, this required unanimous consent of the House or majority approval after clearance by the Rules Committee. The final change did away with the delaying tactic of requesting an "engrossed" copy of a bill. Previously, members could request such a copy that required special paper and printing, often delaying consideration of a bill by several days.

These changes, along with an increase in Democratic representation on committees, had the effect of institutionalizing the mandate beyond the transient effect in voting behavior of the members. They gave the Johnson administration and its allies in Congress the tools to bypass the opposition of Southern Democrats, particularly on civil rights provisions. The institutional changes reflected the extent to which the policy interests of the Great Society coincided with the majority party interests in Congress. Presidents and their advisors have long recognized that their influence decreases with time, an effect heightened by the transient nature of the mandate perception (Light 1999). The mandate might buy short-lived support, but institutional changes can extend this through the entire Congress. This set of unusual tactics allowed the mandate party to permanently strengthen its hand for the battles that would come long after the 1964 election result was forgotten.

5.1.3 1981: A Revolution Without a Majority

The congressional Democrats of 1965 had a significant advantage compared to the Republicans of 1981; they controlled both chambers of Congress and by significant margins. Rules matter more in the House and in 1981 the conservative mandate faced a House controlled by Democrats. The mandate helped give the Republicans control of the Senate, but divided government altered the nature of mandate politics. Divided government is a common theme today, but in 1981 it was new. The 97th Congress was the first to have divided control of the two chambers since 1932, and this ensured that mandate politics would face partisan skirmishes no matter the strength of the conservative signal sent by the election returns.

Divided government meant that the Reagan revolution had to rely on the mandate effect to get through the House. The resulting strategy was to move quickly, rely on the Senate to pass bills in order to pressure the House, and to make use of conservative Democrats and other members voting more conservatively than normal to get past the Democratic leadership. The Democrats recognized that they had to work with Reagan or they risked continued electoral defeat and possibly the loss of the House. On the opening day of the session House Speaker Tip O'Neill admitted as much.

House Democrats, he said,

intend to adapt to changed circumstances, to seek common ground with the other body and the new President. When differences occur we will air them in an atmosphere of constructive dialog rather than partisan recrimination. (*New York Times*, Jan. 6, 1981, p. A1)

Much as President Johnson promised restraint in 1965, O'Neill promised cooperation in 1981. Just as Johnson's restraint quickly gave way to institutional maneuvers to ensure passage of the mandate, O'Neill's cooperation quickly gave way to institutional efforts to block, or at least slow, the Reagan mandate.

On the very day O'Neill offered his cooperation, he led the Democratic majority in rejecting Republican efforts to change rules and committees to help put the mandate into law. The Republican efforts and the Democratic response reflect the competing interests of Schickler's (2001) "disjointed pluralism" model of institutional change. That model suggests that an influx of new Republicans, bolstering the minority's strength, should have led the GOP to seek increased access to institutional positions. Moreover, as the policy interests of the mandate aligned with the minority instead of the majority, we should expect reform efforts designed to overcome the majority party's interest. The

Democrats, in contrast, were apt to seek changes to protect a slim majority, one subject to internal ideological divisions with the increased power of conservative Southern Democrats.

This is precisely what both sides did. In an effort designed to ease the construction of a Republican-conservative Southern Democrat coalition, the Republicans sought greater representation on the all-important Rules and Ways and Means Committees. They wanted the committee ratios to revert from a two to one Democratic advantage to a three to two ratio that better reflected the fact that Republicans now controlled 44 percent of the seats in the chamber. The Democrats refused to give up ratios that gave them close to 66 percent of the seats on the committees, 10 percent more than they held in the House (*New York Times*, Jan. 6, 1981, p. A1). Republican House Member Trent Lott summed up the strategy, noting that the proposed ratios were a 'blatant attempt to block and obstruct Reagan's economic package" (*New York Times*, Jan. 29, 1981, p. A14).

The partisan battle continued over House rules changes. Knowing that the Reagan revolution would be fought through budgetary politics, Republicans sought a House rule that would limit spending to a steadily declining percentage of the Gross National Product. More important, they sought to remove from the Rules Committee jurisdiction regarding floor presentation of budget bills. After easily defeating the Republican proposals, the Democrats enacted rule changes to give the Speaker additional powers to control floor debates and votes. The rules changes gave the Speaker increased flexibility when dealing with quorum calls designed to disrupt House proceedings, the clustering of votes under suspended rule (a move that could hinder Republican efforts to attach riders to bills), and dealing with continuing budget resolutions (*Congressional Quarterly Almanac* 1981).

The rule changes enacted in 1981 look minor compared to those of 1965. The change reflects the fact that the Reagan revolution was not accompanied by the institutional control that the Democrats enjoyed when enacting the Great Society. Given its minority status, Republican Party efforts in the 97th House had to be symbolic. Democratic efforts to use rule changes to derail the mandate had to be tempered. The Democrats had to accommodate the number of members voting more conservatively than normal and to avoid the political risks that would come from being seen as obstructing the Reagan program. The pattern would reverse itself again in 1995 when a new conservative mandate would have the institutional control the Republicans lacked in 1981.

5.1.4 1995: Preparing to Pass the Contract

January 4, 1995, was a nostalgic day for Democratic Rep. Sidney Yates (IL). On that day, the Republicans took control of the House for first time in forty years. Serving also on the last day of GOP control, Representative Yates was the only member of the House around to see both days. The eighty-five-year-old Yates was the only Democrat to have previously served in a Republican-controlled House. None of the Republicans taking their seats that day in the 104th had ever served in a House their own party controlled (*Washington Post*, Nov. 10, 1994, p. A27). That day was as important for the Republicans as it was nostalgic for Rep. Yates. And they were ready.

In the summer of 1994, Newt Gingrich may not have known he was leading the Republicans to a fifty-two-seat gain and with it, control of the House, but he set about planning to implement the Republican agenda anyway. He gathered a team to plan reforms of the House that would help carry out the Contract with America (Wilcox 1995). The reforms they planned would strengthen the Republican leadership and would come to be seen as, "the broadest changes in House committees in almost 50 years" (*Washington Post*, Nov. 17, 1994, p. A1), and "the most sweeping reforms since the 1946 Legislative Reorganization Act" (Wilcox 1995, p. 37).

Gingrich would go further than reorganizing committees. The mandate perception centered on Gingrich and the Contract, so like the leadership supporting the victorious presidents in 1965 and 1981, he sought to institutionalize his power. He took additional steps to centralize power in the Speaker's Office and to ensure that he could move legislation through the House with little interference. The moves led commentators to compare Gingrich to the dominant speakers of days gone by. A commentator in the *New York Times* captured the predominant view well:

The way Newt Gingrich is consolidating power, he is about to become the strongest Speaker of the House since Thomas Brackett Reed and Joseph G. Cannon around the turn of the 20th century and possibly even since the great Henry Clay in the early days of the Republic. (David Rosenbaum, *New York Times*, Dec. 4, 1994, p. 32)

The House Republicans promised to enact the Contract with America in the first 100 days of the 104th Congress. To do so would require a unified party and rules changes to ensure that politics as usual did not derail the Contract. Among the Republican promises was a commitment to allow more open rules for the consideration of legislation on the House floor. The tension between calls for a more open and democratic House and a desire to drive an ideological agenda through the chamber would plague the GOP's efforts throughout the Congress. The mandate perception gave the Republicans strong political and institutional leverage against President Clinton, but, in face of the presidential veto, use of that leverage was conditional on strong victories in Congress. The House also needed to stake out strong conservative positions, given the need to negotiate with a Senate that, although controlled by Republicans, was more narrowly divided and more moderate.

A three-part strategy emerged to both meet the promise of opening up the House and the need to push legislation through it. The institutionalization of the mandate would involve efforts to ensure that the Speaker had influence throughout the chamber, to change the formal rules to support a stronger leadership, and to reduce the power of the opposition.

It was clear early on that Newt Gingrich would not be the kind of Speaker who wanted to facilitate the passage of other people's bills. Rather, he would play a key role in shaping and directing the Republican agenda. His central effort was directed at shaping the jurisdiction and leadership of the House committees. The Republican caucus gave the Speaker-elect the ability to appoint twelve of the twenty-three members of the Steering Committee that would name the committee chairs and along with it the right to name the chair of the Rules Committee. Gingrich moved to control the selection of the committee chairs by announcing his personal choices before the Steering Committee met and by noting his willingness to remove chairs who did not support his legislation (Wilcox 1995). Gingrich bypassed seniority and supported members who shared his conservative positions. He passed over ranking members on Judiciary, Energy and Commerce, and Appropriations (*New York Times*, Nov. 17, 1994, p. 1A). Many saw this as an effort to continue to curry favor with the more recently elected Republicans. Many of them were highly supportive of Gingrich, often believing they owed their electoral success to his leadership.

The most significant rules changes were predicated on the grounds of reducing the bureaucratic structure of the committee system. More important, they reduced the power of committee chairs vis-à-vis the Speaker. Term limits were imposed on both committee and subcommittee chairs. Beyond limiting a member's ability to control a policy area, this also had the effect of more quickly opening leadership positions to younger members, reflecting the desire of the younger members to improve their positions within the institution (Schickler 2001). The powers of the chairs were further reduced by the elimination of proxy voting. Chairs would no longer be able to conduct business without members present and would be unable to mark up legislation using prearranged proxy votes. Committee staff positions were cut by one-third, removing a key resource for chairs in developing policy and drafting legislation. Finally, the promise of more open rules for floor debate meant that chairs lost the opportunity to use restrictive rules to protect their versions of key bills. The Rules Committee (controlled by the Speaker) and the larger membership more generally would have the ability to more easily modify committee bills.

The changes went beyond the operation of committees. Several operational changes targeted opponents of the Republican agenda. Three committees with nominally Democratic constituencies – District of Columbia, Merchant Marine and Fisheries, and Post Office and Civil Service – were eliminated. The most controversial, if largely symbolic, change was a rule requiring a supermajority to enact most tax increases. Although this change clearly reduced the ability of lawmakers to increase revenues, few thought it realistic that the Republicans would seek tax increases of any kind. A more significant change came when the Republicans abolished direct funding of Legislative Service Organizations or caucuses that provided information and visibility for groups of like-minded legislators. Although Republicans argued the groups were unnecessary bureaucracy and beholden to special interests, the most prominent of them – the Black Caucus, the Congressional Hispanic Caucus, and the Caucus for Women's Issues – were heavily Democratic (*Washington Post*, Dec. 7, 1994, p. A1). The funds allocated to the groups were redirected to general operations funds so the groups could continue, but members would have to divert office funds to support them.

In the 104th Congress, the House of Representatives would operate differently. The differences were not minor, but nor were they earth-shattering. The result was an institution that was supportive of a strong Speaker, a unified party, and the conservative mandate that would come to influence member voting over the following weeks and months. There also were efforts to decentralize power within the institution, partly in response to the large freshman class.

5.1.5 Mandates and Study of Institutional Change

Across the three mandated Congresses, we see efforts to match political gain with institutional power. The more extensive changes were seen in 1965 and 1995 when the policy interests supported by the mandate coincided with both the House majority party's interests, and the desire of new members swept into office by the mandate surge for access to institutional power. In both of these years political observers and scholars noted the historical character of the changes, with both likened to the times of powerful speakers at the turn of the century. The nature of the changes seen in all three of the years closely follow the expectations developed from existing literature on institutional change, so we can ask whether these years are different from years with no mandate election. The answer is yes and no.

To get a sense of how institutional politics in mandated Congresses differed from nonmandate years, we examined *Congressional Quarterly Almanac* from 1965 to 2002, recording all instances of changes in rules, procedure, or organization.[4] We focused on changes related to the enactment of policy, including rules in the House, procedural changes, committee procedures and structure, and organizational changes. We then used the discussion in *Congressional Quarterly* to assess the extent of the change, simply coding each year as exhibiting no significant change, limited change, moderate change, or major change

---

[4] We examined each annual edition from 1965 to 2002, covering both sessions from the 89th to the 107th Congress. Although rule changes and organizational bills are most often passed in the first session of a Congress, the occasional reform bill is passed in the second session. We read through and noted changes in both the initial chapter that reviews the previous election and entire session of Congress, and in later years we examined the chapter on congressional affairs.

TABLE 5.1. *The Extent of Congressional Rule Changes, 1965–2002*

Extent of Change	First Session		Second Session	
	Number	Percent	Number	Percent
None	6	32	15	79
Limited	6	32	2	11
Moderate	4	21	2	11
Major	3	16	0	0

Source: *Congressional Quarterly Almanac* and Schickler (2000).

depending on the historical nature of the change.[5] The results of this quick analysis are presented in Table 5.1.

Mandate years are not unique in witnessing institutional change. Roughly 70 percent of all Congresses make changes in the first session with close to a third enacting either major or moderate amount of change. Where mandated, Congresses may be unique is in the amount of change. Two of the three years coded as enacting major changes followed the mandates of 1964 and 1994. The remaining year with major change was 1975 in the aftermath of the Democrats' post-Watergate gains. In that year Congress eliminated proxy voting in Congress, changed the cloture threshold to sixty votes, and the Democrats switched to a Steering Committee to name committee chairs. The 97th Congress in 1981 was coded as having no significant changes, an understandable result given the competing interests at work that session.

Mandates appear to have the potential to strongly connect the interests of a majority with the policy interests of a large number of members of Congress, thus facilitating significant change. In 1965 and 1995, the combination of interests put in place the circumstances that would allow for the passage of Schickler's "common carriers," a package of reforms that jointly serve a combination of interests within Congress. Institutional change was limited in 1981 as a result of a decoupling of the policy interests and the interest of the majority Democrats.

---

[5] As a precaution, we checked our list against the list of significant partisan changes developed by Schickler (2000). Between 1965 and 1995, he found thirteen years with a significant change. All thirteen were included in our list and we had six coded as limited change, four as moderate, and three as major change. That list is an expanded version of Binder's (1996), so we believe we have accounted for all the major changes if not properly assessed their scope.

Two of our cases thus appear to be special instances of where political forces come together to disrupt the status quo of the institution.
The third produced a more competitive environment as a result of the
occurrence of divided government. All of the institutional battles described here were fought with the goal of enacting, or defeating, the
mandate policy agenda. To determine the impact of the mandate perception on the policy battles we need to look past the organizational
battles of the first few days to the rest of the session.

We now ask to what extent the mandate perceptions altered
not the internal workings of Congress but the policy outputs they
produced.

5.2   TURNING THE MANDATE OFF

To gauge direct policy consequences, we must isolate the influence
of the mandate consensus from other influences on policy making.
We do so through a counterfactual analysis. History provides us
the knowledge of what happened in the Congresses under the mandate
effect. The counterfactual analysis asks what Congress might have done
if the mandate had not existed. In simpler terms, we turn the mandate
off and ask, what would have been the likely outcome of congressional
votes under politics as usual?

An example from our opening story best illustrates our procedure.
In 1965, the liberal mandate from the 1964 election sweep was in full
effect. President Johnson and his allies in the Senate were working to
enact the Voting Rights Act. Knowing that the bill would pass, opponents sought to reduce its effectiveness by attaching amendments that
would limit the government's ability to enforce the new voting rights
in the states. Among these attempts was a Republican amendment to
limit the United States Attorney General's ability to bring lawsuits to
enforce the act. States' rights Republicans and Southern Democrats
knew that state attorneys general would be far less likely to enforce
the laws and so they sought to effectively gut the bill by excluding the
federal government from enforcement activities. The amendment came
to a vote in roll call number 59 of 1965, and the conservatives lost.
The amendment was defeated by a vote of forty-four to thirty-four
and the stronger version of the Voting Rights Act went on to become
a keystone of the Great Society. But how would the Voting Rights Act
have fared absent the perception on Capitol Hill that the Democratic

sweep of the 1964 elections carried a message of voter endorsement of civil rights?

Our logic requires us to know how liberal or conservative a particular roll call was. We observe that from the vote margin. On a very liberal measure, for example, we would expect to see a small number of the most liberal members voting against a large block of conservatives, moderates, and even moderate liberals. In contrast, a vote won by the liberal side with a lop-sided majority is probably not very liberal. Why else would moderates and moderate conservatives cross over? To produce a summary measure for each vote, we array all members actually voting on a particular roll call from right to left and then solve for the cut point which would reproduce the actual outcome on the assumption that all less liberal members vote the conservative position and all more liberal members vote the liberal position.[6]

Then we ask "what if?" What if the mandate perception had not existed? That is the same as asking what would the outcome have been if members had voted their normal position on the left-right scale (as opposed to the early session deviation in the direction of the mandate). We estimate normal ideological position from our end of the session grand cumulation of each member's votes.[7] Now we simulate each of the roll call votes by applying the estimated cut point – essentially how liberal you have to be to take the liberal side – to the normal distribution of positions. For each vote, two outcomes are possible. The vote may turn out as it actually did, but with the sizes of majority and minority somewhat altered. Or, the case of our focus to come, it may be reversed, the winning majority reduced so much that it is no longer a majority and measures that passed now fail or those that failed now pass. These we call "counterfactual reversals." They are outcomes that would have been different under the counterfactual of no mandate influence.[8]

---

[6] The cut point is then the midpoint between the most liberal member voting on the conservative side and the least liberal member voting the liberal side. The personal ideological position measures are taken from the vote block in which the particular roll call occurred. Recall that "position" is not quite "ideology" because we believe that position reflects a strategic accommodation of true personal preference (ideology) with perceived electoral expedience. Thus, members do not become more liberal or conservative under the mandate influence, but their voting patterns do.

[7] That is expected to have a modest bias in the direction of the mandate because it includes the early session votes that deviate toward mandate.

[8] Another way to think of the counterfactual is that it expresses the expected outcome of actual votes as if they had been held not when they were, but on the last day of the session.

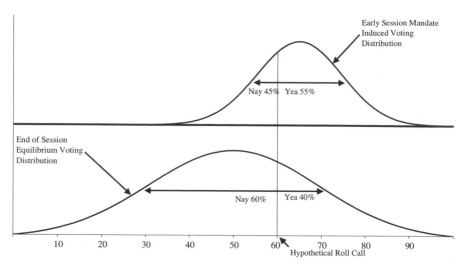

FIGURE 5.1. Illustration of the Counterfactual Procedure: A Hypothetical Roll Call.

We illustrate the procedure for a hypothetical roll call in Figure 5.1. Imagine that we have a roll call that cuts the current distribution early in the session (on top) at sixty on a hypothetical left-to-right scale. Because the voting distribution is shifted to the right for a conservative mandate (as in 1981 and 1995) the particular roll call divides the distribution such that 55 percent vote yea (conservative) and 45 percent nay (liberal). Then we ask the counterfactual, what if the distribution looked like the end of the session equilibrium (on the bottom)? There we see that exactly the same issue would have divided the votes such that the yea side now loses with only 40 percent of the votes and the nay side wins with 60 percent. This is a counterfactual reversal, an outcome that would have been different if the mandate influence were not present early in the session when the vote was taken.

For the case of the Voting Rights amendment attempt we pose the counterfactual question, what would the outcome of this particular vote have been if members had been voting as they normally did, without the surge of extra liberalism of the first weeks of the 89th Congress. We again array the members from right to left and all those more liberal than seventy-one become "nay" voters and those less liberal become "yea" voters.

The answer is that it would have been different. With the mandate "turned off," forty-one Senators had liberalism propensities less than 71 percent and thus should have voted to gut the Voting Rights Act. The 44–34 liberal victory becomes, absent the mandate, a 37–41 loss. Under the counterfactual, the outcome on this roll call is reversed. The implication is striking and illustrative of the policy impact of the mandate perception. The Democratic gains from the 1964 election in the relatively conservative Senate were not enough to pass the Voting Rights Act in its strong form. Absent the mandate effect, blacks across the South may not have had the opportunity to use the ballot box as a new weapon in the fight for civil rights. The Voting Rights Act, as passed, would lead to a new generation of black elected officials. It would add a large number of Democratic voters to the electorate. And it would change America's political parties. From that point on, the Democratic Party would be the party of racial liberalism and black voters would be a core component of the Democratic coalition (Carmines and Stimson 1989). Without the influence of a perceived 1964 mandate, none of this would have been.

The policy implications of mandates become more striking when we look across all three mandate years and perform a similar analysis for all roll calls. Absent the perception of mandate, much of what defined the Great Society and the Reagan revolution would not have come to pass, and what did come of the Contract with America would have been even less. Here we take up the three cases in order and estimate what might have been without the influence of mandate perceptions.

5.2.1 The Great Society of 1964–1965

The aftermath of the 1964 election, particularly in the House, is the worst case for mandate influence. The influx of liberal Democrats into the 89th Congress restricted the number of members who were likely to respond to the mandate perception by voting even more liberally than normal. The large majorities the Democrats enjoyed in each chamber made the institution so liberal that further changes were hard to find. Nevertheless, we have already seen that replacement effects were not enough to ensure passage of the Voting Rights Act in the Senate.

TABLE 5.2. *Summary of Counterfactual Analyses – 89th Congress*

	House		Senate	
	Mandate Politics	Normal Voting	Mandate Politics	Normal Voting
Average Split (Liberal-Conservative)	238–146	238–146	53–47	50–50
Liberal Wins	85.2%	80.7%	79.7%	74.1%
Liberal Position Gains	60.0%		65.7%	
Counterfactual Reversals	6		7	

Note: Liberal position gains show the percentage of roll calls in which the liberal side gained from the mandate.

Summary. Table 5.2 offers a summary of our counterfactual analyses for the 1965 session. For our full session averages we display two conditions, "mandate politics" – the historical roll call outcomes – and "normal voting" – the counterfactual outcomes based on normal voting patterns. In simpler terms they are "what happened?" and "what might have happened?" These averages understate true effects because they cover the full session, whereas the mandate decays throughout the session.

For the 1965 House of Representatives what did happen and what might have are the same; there is no mandate effect, at least on the size of the liberal and conservative blocks. This is a handy, if unintended, demonstration that our counterfactual analysis does not create spurious differences when there is no effect to "turn off." By another measure, how often the liberal side prevails under the two conditions, there is an effect; an 85 percent liberal win rate is reduced to about 80 percent with the mandate turned off. We also assess which side gains or loses from the mandate effect. For the House, the liberal side gains votes about 60 percent of the time and loses the other 40 percent, an unimpressive showing.

For the Senate, in contrast, the estimated effect of the mandate is that about three votes are shifted from the conservative side to the liberal side. (Or, if we restricted analysis to the mandate period, the effect would be about twice that.) The liberal win rate is reduced by about 6 percent when the mandate is turned off and about two-thirds of the time simulated changes benefit the liberal mandate coalition. We will see later that although relatively few votes turn out differently than they might have, those few are pretty important.

The Substance. The full list of votes from 1965 that turned out different in the counterfactual situation is presented in an appendix to this chapter, in Table 5.5. In the 89th House, three votes stand out. Roll call 3, part of the Democrats' effort to alter House rules to strengthen the power of the majority party, was a key vote by *Congressional Quarterly's* estimation (as well as ours). The rule changes allowed the Democrats to ensure consideration of the Great Society even as the mandate perception faded. Two other votes played a key role in Democratic legislation, one ensuring a vote to create the Department of Housing and Urban Development, the second defeating a Republican effort to derail the Equal Employment Opportunity Act.

The Senate witnessed more important changes as a result of mandate politics. Nearly a quarter of the Senate voted more liberal than might be expected through late February and fourteen Senators remained influenced by the mandate well into May. The impact can be seen in the votes that might have been reversed absent the mandate. In addition to the federal enforcement provision, the mandate effect was central in defeating an effort to ensure that federal courts in Southern states would hear cases brought under the Voting Rights Act. This was an effort to place enforcement in the hands of white Southern judges predominantly put in place before the civil rights movement. Both amendments had the potential to derail the Voting Rights bill by placing oversight in the hands of Southern officials who were part of the governing elite, which maintained the existing racially exclusive system.

The mandate also helped ensure defeat of an effort to gut antipoverty programs by providing governors with veto power over their use. The remaining reversals had the potential to affect President Johnson's foreign policy, and in particular his efforts to direct economic aid to Southeast Asia at the outset of America's involvement in Vietnam.

5.2.2   The Reagan Revolution of 1980–1981

The power of the mandate message is at its greatest in 1981. Following the stunning Republican wins of 1980, many members of both houses of Congress departed from their normal voting strategies to heed the conservative message. Over 200 members were still showing mandate effects in June of 1981, six months into the 97th Congress. The policy impact identified by the counterfactual analysis is equally striking. This has to be the case, for the conservative Republican president achieved

TABLE 5.3. *Summary of Counterfactual Analyses – 97th Congress*

	House		Senate	
	Mandate Politics	Normal Voting	Mandate Politics	Normal Voting
Average Split (Liberal-Conservative)	183–218	192–208	38–56	41–53
Conservative Wins	61.1%	58.0%	83.6%	72.1%
Conservative Position Gains	68.8%		77.9%	
Counterfactual Reversals	6		28	

Note: Conservative position gains show the percentage of roll calls in which the conservative side gained from the mandate.

brief legislative dominance with a small majority in the Senate and a House controlled by the Democrats.

Summary. The impact of the mandate on Reagan's legislative success is evident when we look across all roll calls for 1981. The summary figures are presented in Table 5.3. Of particular note is the change in average conservative votes in the House. Under normal politics, conservatives still out polled liberals, but on average they would not have reached a majority. With the mandate perception in place, the conservative average increases to 218 votes, the slimmest majority possible. Although slim, this majority combined with a sizable increase in the average conservative winning margin to ensure passage of Reagan's agenda in a chamber controlled by the opposition. The equally slim Republican majority in the Senate also benefitted from mandate politics. The conservative side gained votes in close to 80 percent of the roll calls, winning an additional 11 percent. The strong impact in the Senate is also evident when we consider the votes where the outcome might have been reversed under normal voting. Our analysis identified twenty-eight votes that might have been affected, spanning the entire year.

The Substance. We focus here on the central elements of the Reagan revolution. The full set of possible reversals is listed in the appendix in Table 5.6. Little that defines the legacy of Ronald Reagan is left untouched by removing the mandate effect. Perhaps most important are critical votes on Reagan's efforts to reshape the federal government through cuts in social programs, reduced taxes, and increased defense spending. All of these efforts benefitted from the mandate consensus. Without it, the House would not have adopted Reagan's budget targets or allowed for more military construction. Senate Democrats would have succeeded in altering Reagan's reductions to President Carter's final budget, his new budget targets, and his cuts in housing, food stamps, and taxes.

Beyond the fiscal bills, the mandate effect allowed Reagan to win higher spending for controversial weapons systems such as the B-1 bomber and the MX nuclear missile. The mandate even ensured Senate support for Reagan's effort to sell AWACS radar planes to Saudi Arabia. In short, the Reagan revolution, in both domestic and foreign policy, would have been no revolution absent the mandate effect we document. Reagan did not have enough conservative votes to pass his program. He needed "temporary" conservatives under early session mandate influence to build majorities for his tax and spending cuts. Late in the year he needed mandate induced votes to ensure that his defense buildup would be enacted.

5.2.3 The Contract with America, 1994–1995

The election of 1994 presents a similar problem to that of 1964. The dramatic Republican gains, culminating in the complete takeover of Congress, put in place one of the most conservative Congresses in history. The likely outcome is that conservative majorities would be bolstered by the mandate, not created by it.

Summary. The mandate, however, still had an impact beyond the replacement effects caused by the Republican surge. Table 5.4 presents a summary of our analysis of the year's roll calls. Conservatives in the House witnessed only marginal gains, gaining votes on just over half of the roll calls and seeing their average victory margin improve by twelve votes. The Senate saw a stronger impact. The average number of conservative votes increased to fifty-six, just shy of the sixty necessary for cloture. Senate conservatives gained votes on over two-thirds of the roll calls, helping them win an additional 10 percent of the votes.

The Substance. The 104th Congress saw a large number of votes that may have turned out differently had the mandate not existed. Much

TABLE 5.4. *Summary of Counterfactual Analyses – 104th Congress*

	House		Senate	
	Mandate Politics	Normal Voting	Mandate Politics	Normal Voting
Average Split (Liberal-Conservative)	170–251	175–245	42–56	45–53
Conservative Wins	85.5%	81.2%	81.0%	71.0%
Conservative Position Gains	55.5%		70.0%	
Counterfactual Reversals	26		41	

Note: Conservative position gains show the percentage of roll calls in which the conservative side gained from the mandate.

of the Contract with America did not become law, but the mandate affected what did, and it had a significant impact on the bills the Republican Congress passed and then used to confront President Clinton. The mandate altered the bargaining situation during a period of bitterly divided government.

The effects go further. The mandate shaped the course of politics and policy making yet to come. Whereas we focus on the Contract as the signature legislation of the 104th Congress, it is far from the only impact that is discernible. Having won control of both chambers, Republicans sought other policy changes through legislation and budget negotiations. The full effect of the mandate can be seen in the appendix in Table 5.7, in which we list the votes that were reversed in the counterfactual analysis.

The centerpiece of the 104th Congress was the Contract, the national campaign that many credit as a driving factor behind the Republican takeover of Congress. Seven of the ten items in the Contract were affected by the mandate, almost always making the items more conservative by defeating Democratic amendments or accepting Republican ones. One item, regulatory reform, was signed into law by the president. Three items – welfare reform, middle class tax cuts, and tort reform – passed both chambers only to be vetoed. Congress overrode the veto of the tort reform measure, a major Republican victory.

One vote deserves special mention because it helps illustrate the impact of the mandate even as bills go down to defeat. On March 22, 1995, the House passed a resolution to consider the sweeping reform provisions that would have removed entitlement from federal welfare policies. Welfare reform did not become law in 1995, but this vote ensured that it became a major agenda item. Moreover, the Republican bill that passed both chambers shaped the debate surrounding the bill in 1996. The mandate effect shaped the bill that won wide support in Congress, support that forced a Democratic president to alter one of the major tenets of the Great Society. It took a mandate to undo a mandate.

Looking beyond the Contract, the mandate allowed the Republicans to defeat Democratic efforts to restore funding to education programs and the Public Broadcasting System, to reduce funding for a national missile defense system, to kill energy development in the Artic National Wildlife Refuge, and to amend a bill to ban partial birth abortion. The mandate also affected bills changing the Clean Water Act, solid waste cleanup, antiterrorism efforts, and the congressional version of the federal budget. Perhaps most significant, at least retrospectively, was the impact of the mandate on the passage of the Telecommunication Deregulation Act, which absent the mandate, may have been tabled by Democrats. That law altered federal rules for media ownership, the regulation of wireless technology, and other communications services.

5.2.4   A Validity Check

In the end, it is reasonable to ask just how confident we are that these votes matter. We have demonstrated through the counterfactual analysis that the mandates we identify influenced outcomes of congressional roll calls on key issues, but are these roll calls important? For several reasons, we believe they are.

To begin the assessment, it is useful to distinguish between votes and bills. Important bills usually have multiple votes and it is often the case that the vote on final passage is not close. Thus, in the counterfactual analysis, we don't often encounter bills that would not have passed. Instead, like the Voting Rights example, we witness close votes on amendments that would have been reversed without the influence of mandates. The question then becomes, are these votes important ones?

We can compare our votes to those identified by *Congressional Quarterly* (CQ) as key votes. This provides a validity check on our assessment, one that uses a widely used authoritative source on what votes and bills were important in a given Congress. There are three possibilities. The vote in question may have been CQ's key vote. Second, it may be on a bill identified as "key," but not CQ's choice as the most important vote. Or third, it may be on a measure that didn't make the key list.

Appendix Table 5.8 presents such a comparison. The first column of the table lists actual CQ key votes that were reversed in our analysis. The second column lists bills that were the subject of CQ key votes and counterfactual reversals, but where the reversed vote was not the one CQ designated "key." Among the reversals we record are five CQ key votes and nineteen bills that were the subject of key votes. Mandate perceptions altered voting on many of the most important policy issues addressed in these years. The importance of these issues extends far beyond the individual Congresses within which they took place; these issues define many of the important shifts in American politics over the last forty years.

5.3   MANDATES AND THE FLOW OF PUBLIC POLICY

So far, we have documented the impact of mandate politics on Congressional operations and the outcome of legislative roll calls. But the impact of mandates goes further, touching on much that is important in understanding policy change. The three periods we look at – the Great Society, the Reagan revolution, and the Gingrich Contract with America – are instances of significant policy change. They differ from normal depictions of the policy process, depictions often characterized as incremental, or worse, gridlocked. The result of these bursts of policy making is well documented: the modern welfare state and entitlement programs, major civil rights bills, a new defense buildup, major tax cuts, reductions in social spending, and the ending of welfare as we know it. But how can mandates help us understand not just the behavior of individual members of Congress and chamber medians, but the entire policy system?

Part of the answer lays in the mandate's influence on the federal policy agenda. Jones (1999) argues that elections matter to the extent that they alter the relative bargaining position of the president and Congress in a separation of powers game. For Jones, significant policy change is likely when there is agenda congruity across the institutions of government. Agenda congruity requires three things: (1) the president and congressional leaders must agree on the basic ideological premises of policy solutions that are acceptable to the public; (2) national political actors must be responsive to changes in national politics; and (3) there must be a strong base of support in Congress for the recognized policy solutions. This is precisely what characterizes mandate politics.

Mandates begin with an electoral surge that provides a strong base within Congress (in two instances unified control). A consensus regarding the direction of public preferences forms. Then elites respond by altering their behavior in the direction of the changes, thus providing additional support within Congress. The result is a shift in how Congress processes issues.

Agenda studies often portray a process where issues are processed serially, tackled one at a time as a result of limited attention and resources (Jones 1994; Wood and Peake 1998). The agenda congruity produced by mandates puts in place the conditions for parallel processing. Policy activity occurs across a wide range of issues as Congress acts on the policy proposals associated with the mandate story. A brief look at the bills influenced by the mandate can demonstrate the breadth of the issues addressed. The 89th Congress addressed issues ranging from housing, Appalachian development, and civil rights, to healthcare, international development, and foreign aid. The Reagan budgets left few issue areas untouched. And the 104th Congress dealt with issues as far ranging as crime, tort reform, the United Nations, education funds, missile defense, abortion, and telecommunications.

These influences parallel a change in the conditions promoting what some have called conditional party governance (see Binder 1996, 1997; see also Aldrich and Rhode 2000). Mandates have the effect of putting in place relatively unified and ideologically similar congressional parties, which also benefit from the temporary support of those influenced by the mandate effect. These conditions have been associated not only with changes in agenda setting but also instances where Congress can overcome the gridlock that has characterized recent decades (Binder 1999). The ideological convergence of the actors through both replacement effects and the mandate influence meant that not only were many items placed on the agenda, but many also became law.

For evidence of these bursts in policy activity we can look to the number of major laws passed in each Congress. For data we turn to Erikson, MacKuen, and Stimson's (2002) coding of the important laws identified by Mayhew (1991).[9] For each Congress, these authors counted major

---

[9] The list of important laws has regularly been updated using a list of sources comparable to those in Mayhew's (1991) original study. Erikson, MacKuen, and Stimson (2002) combine the original and updated lists to cover a wider time period.

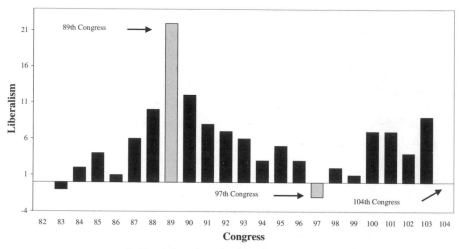

FIGURE 5.2. Policy Liberalism by Congress, 82–104 (1951–1996).

liberal laws as +1 and major conservative laws as a −1. Laws designated by Mayhew (and for later years, Erikson et al.) as exceptionally important are double counted as a +2 or −2 respectively. The final measure is the sum of liberal minus conservative counts. The biennial data for each Congress is displayed in Figure 5.2.

The mandate congresses (in gray) stand out for several reasons.

- The Great Society 89th Congress stands above all others in terms of productivity. Its twenty-two pieces of liberal legislation dwarfs the next highest (twelve in the following Congress) and the average of the remaining years, a far more incremental value of four.
- Not surprisingly, the conservative mandates stand out for the opposite reason, replacing liberal lawmaking with conservative action. The 97th Congress is one of only two to exhibit a conservative total, and the first one since the beginning of the Eisenhower Administration.
- The 104th Congress again reverses a trend of accumulating liberal laws, producing a combination of laws that resulted in no net liberalism. (It is invisible in the figure because its net value is zero.) Here we see a Congress bent on legislating a conservative mandate up against a president determined not to let that happen. The resulting standoff is a gain for conservatism, relative to other congresses.

The mandate dynamic offers a picture of the conditions necessary for significant policy change. These conditions also appear to play a role in the larger trends in American politics and public policy. The stories of shifting electorates and the changes in roll call behavior give way to new political forces that sometimes add to the mandate impact and at other times reverse it.

But the American electorate has a knack for correcting the excesses of politicians, so a response to the changes brought by the mandate seems likely. That brings us to the story of what happens as the mandate fades and the question of how the public and the winners and losers respond. We take up that story in our next chapter.

5.4 APPENDIX

TABLE 5.5. *Counterfactual Reversals – 89th Congress*

Roll Call	Content
House of Representatives	
3	Order the question; to revise the House rules to strengthen the majority.
80	Reject GOP motion to recommit HUD creation bill.
113	Accept Democratic amendment to DC insurance bill.
115	Accept Democratic amendment to public works bill.
146	Table motion to reconsider GOP open rule for EEOA.
U.S. Senate	
20	Accept Democratic amendment to Inter-American Development Bank bill.
33	Table GOP amendment to Foreign Agents Registration Act.
56	Reject GOP amendment to Voting Rights Act to limit Attorney General Actions.
64	Reject Southern Democratic amendment to give discretion to federal courts located in the states where action is taken under Voting Rights Act.
87	Accept Democratic amendment to Foreign Assistance Act to increase economic aid to southeast Asia.
92	Reject Southern Democratic amendment to Foreign Assistance Act.
191	Reject GOP amendment to Economic Opportunity Act to give governors veto authority over antipoverty programs.

TABLE 5.6. *Counterfactual Reversals – 97th Congress*

Roll Call	Content
	House of Representatives
30–31 34	Accept GOP amendment to Reagan budget targets, adopt the targets, and GOP instructions to conferees.
54	Concur with GOP amend re: staff levels at NOAA.
55	Reject Democratic amendment to reduce military construction.
108	Reject Democratic effort to review MX placement.
	U.S. Senate
43 44 47 67 68 76	Reject Democratic amendment to Reagan budget revisions.
92 94 96 109	Reject Democratic amendment to Reagan budget targets.
128	Reject GOP amendment to defense appropriation.
137	Reject Democratic amendment to increase housing funding.
145	Reject Democratic amendment to allow for adjustments in food stamp.
160 162 164 168 170	Reject Democratic amendment to RR budget reconciliation.
193 207 210 219 224	Reject Democratic amendment to RR tax cut bill.
284	Accept GOP amendment to 1982 appropriations.
319	Accept GOP amendment to foreign aid bill.
334	Defeat Democratic amendment to Dept. of Interior budget.
338	Reject House effort to disapprove AWACS sale.
450	Reject Democratic effort to reduce funds for B-1 and MX.

TABLE 5.7. *Counterfactual Reversals – 104th Congress*

Roll Call	Content
House of Representatives	
86	Rejecting amendment to Line Item Veto.
116	Reject Democratic effort to recommit Violent Criminal Incarceration Act.
120 124	Reject Democratic amendments to crime bill and accept
127	GOP bill.
133	Consider National Security Revitalization Act.
137–141	Reject three and accept two amendments to NSRA.
144	Reject motion to recommit NSRA.
192	Reject Democratic amendment to Regulatory Overhaul bill.
204	Reject GOP amendment to Tort Reform bill.
255	Pass resolution to consider Welfare Reform bill.
290	Resolution to consider CWA Tax Relief Act.
329	Accept GOP amendment to change Clean Water Act.
396	Reject amendment to military construction bill.
U.S. Senate	
68 71	Table Democratic amendment to Balanced Budget Amend.
109 111	Table Democratic amendment to Line Item Veto.
123	Table Democratic amendment to reinstate education funds.
131	Defeat Democratic amendment to restore PBS funding.
135 142	Reject motion to table GOP amendment to Tort Reform bill,
144–146	table two Democratic and accept two GOP amendments.
168	Table Democratic amendment to Solid Waste bill.
192 213	Table two Democratic and accept one GOP amendment to
224	budget.
241	Table Democratic amendment to antiterrorism bill.
252 254–55	Reject two Democratic amendments to Telecommunications Deregulation bill and defeat Democratic effort to table the bill.
289 292	Table one Democratic and one GOP amendment to Tort Reform bill.
302–03 310	Reject Democratic amendment to Regulatory Overhaul bill.
354–55	Table Democratic amendments to reduce Missile Defense funding.
411 441	Table Democratic and accept GOP amend. to Welfare Reform bill.
525	Table Democratic amendment to kill ANWAR development.
532 541 543	Reject Democratic motions 336 to alter the Budget Reconciliation bill.
594	Reject motion to table GOP amendment to Partial Birth Abortion Ban.

TABLE 5.8. *Counterfactual Reversals and Congressional Quarterly Key Votes*

CQ Key Vote	CQ Key Bill But Not Key Vote
1965 House	
HR8 Changes to House Rules HR7984 Delete rent supplements in HUD bill.	
1965 Senate	
	S1564 Voting Rights Act S1837 Foreign Assistance Act HR8283 Economic Opportunity Act
1981 House	
HCR115 1982 Budget Targets	
1981 Senate	
HCR194 AWACS Sale	SCR9 Fiscal 1981 Budget Revisions HR3512 Defense Appropriations HJR266 Reagan Tax Cut Package HJR325 Fiscal 1982 Appropriations HR4995 B-1 and MX Appropriations
1995 House	
HJR73 Term Limits Amendment	HR4 Welfare Reform Bill (CWA*) HR1215 Tax Relief Act (CWA)
1995 Senate	
	HJR1 Balanced Budget Amendment (CWA) S4 Line Item Veto (CWA) HR956 Tort Reform Bill (CWA) S652 Telecommunications Deregulation S440 Highway Funding Bill S343 Regulatory Overhaul Bill (CWA) S1026 National Missile Defense Appropriation HR4 Welfare Reform (CWA) HR1833 Partial Birth Abortion Ban

Note: The asterisk indicates a Contract with America item.

6

The Irresistible Meets the Unmovable

Mandates begin with excitement for the winners and political horror for the losers. They end with the dull thud of reality. "Politics will never be the same again," we all say. And then a few months later it is.

We close our study of the phenomenon in this chapter by taking a hard look at the aftermath. What is politics like when we have reached a consensus that politics has changed and then – with the real experience of several months – bounced back to our previous understanding? We look at the reinterpretation of the signal, how the clarity, once obvious to all, becomes muddled and contentious. And then we close the electoral cycle by looking at the next election, two years after the mandate. The question of focus is whether all that action by politicians to respond appropriately to the mandate signal is rewarded by voters.

6.1 THE RETURN TO NORMAL POLITICS

After a few months into the new Congress, new information flows into the Washington community. New polls are released. Special elections offer a new snapshot of the public. And, perhaps most important, the losing party regroups. Mandate politics are thus transient, a temporary shift in beliefs and behavior subject to new influences. Mandate reactions give way to something else, a return to normal politics. The "irresistible revolution meets the unmovable constitution" (*New York Times*, Dec. 20, 1995, p. B12) was how the *New York Times* put it in its retrospective view of the 104th Congress.

In this chapter, we turn to the time period where the irresistible mandate meets the new information flows, the unmovable institutions of government, and the elections that follow. We look at how the mandate is discussed as the information flow changes and how policy outputs shift as a result. We also ask whether members of Congress are rewarded by voters for responding to the mandate or whether they are punished for their excesses. This last question is an important one from the perspective of the operation of American democracy. If responsive elected officials are not rewarded by voters by being returned to office, then an important incentive to do the public's bidding may be lost. Moreover, if voters are as retrospective as some claim, then the members who respond should be rewarded. If voters are more prospective, the mandate response would be lost, as voters look to the future and focus on dealing with emerging challenges.

6.1.1   The Tide Turns

Electorates have short political memories, and a mandate consensus, no matter how powerful and consequential it may have been, does not appear to lengthen them. By the end of the first session of the mandated Congress – barely a year after the monumental elections – the attention of the media, politicians, and voters in each case had turned elsewhere. By the end of 1965 attention had shifted to Vietnam, civil rights, and the hopes of a Republican recovery in 1966 after Barry Goldwater's campaign was in the past. In 1981, it was the economy and President Reagan's budget director's confessions of a lack of faith in the president's economic program. In 1995, it was warring over the budget and the subsequent government shutdown that dominated the news. In each case, the tilt of news flow was contrary to the direction of the earlier mandate. The tide of political information had turned.

Given the short political memory of voters and the even shorter attention span of the media, it is not surprising that the mandate consensus erodes still further in the following year. To investigate how the mandate was portrayed, we again collected media stories that used the word "mandate." This time we cover the years 1966, 1982, and 1996, and we limited our search to the *New York Times*. The single media outlet is a limitation, but it does provide the means to have an electronically searchable archive for each year. For 1966, we searched

TABLE 6.1. *Mandate Coverage One Year Later: Reinterpreting the Past and Thinking Ahead*

	1966	1982	1996
Previous Mandate Election	21%	17%	12%
(Pro)	(50)	(43)	(27)
(Anti)	(50)	(57)	(73)
Forthcoming Election	32	23	28
Policy Issue	13	22	24
Other	34	38	36
TOTAL	100%	100%	100%
N	38	138	127

Source: ProQuest Historical Newspapers (1966); Lexis/Nexis (1982 and 1996).

historical archives of the *Times* available from ProQuest Historical Newspapers using the terms "landslide" and "mandate." For the two later years, we searched Lexis/Nexis using only "mandate" as a search term.[1] Table 6.1 presents a breakdown of the stories based on the main topic of coverage.

We begin with the stories mentioning the previous mandate election, displayed in the top three rows of the table. The erosion of the mandate consensus is evidenced first by the relatively sparse coverage of the previous election, which is now old news. In 1966, about a fifth of the stories referred to the mandate of 1964, the remainder covered upcoming elections, policy issues, or state and local politics. The percentage of stories referencing past mandates declines as we move forward in time. By 1982, it was down to 17 percent of stories and by 1996 only 12 percent of the mandate related stories are about 1994. The political memory of the press is short and, based on only this slim evidence, appears to have grown shorter over time.

When the press does look back at the previous mandate, it is not likely to be supportive of those in power. We coded each story as to the main thrust of the mandate reference, asking whether it signaled continued support of a mandate interpretation or called it into question. In 1966, the very small number of stories (eight to be exact) split evenly

[1] The different search terms are driven by differences in language use across years, the sources, and the products of the two search engines. The search terms chosen produce the most comparable results.

between being pro- and antimandate. The tone of the coverage grew increasingly negative following the subsequent mandate elections. In 1982, 57 percent of the stories suggested that the Reagan revolution never existed, was overstated, or exhausted. In 1996, the tone was sharply against the mandate, with close to three-quarters of the stories portraying the idea that congressional Republicans had exaggerated, misread or squandered the voters' mandate. Pro-mandate stories were seen across all months of the year, but at no time did they significantly outnumber antimandate stories that tended to become increasingly frequent as the year went on. The aggregate picture of the information flow is not of consensus, but of contention. The once powerful mandate signal became rarely discussed and then often questioned.

The aggregate numbers mask some interesting elements of how mandates are portrayed and used by political actors. The increasingly antimandate tone is likely to be a function of increased partisan battles over the mandate claim. In 1966, our search turned up one instance in which President Johnson asked the American people to renew and continue his mandate. The remaining stories were mainly media commentary on the impact of the landslide, the erosion of support for Johnson, and the impact of Vietnam.

In contrast, the mandate debate in 1982 was both more partisan and more strategic. There were four instances where President Reagan, Vice President Bush, or Reagan's chief of staff made claims of a continuing mandate from 1980. A fifth claim was made by a Republican member of Congress. Given the policy impact of the mandate consensus demonstrated earlier, it makes sense that there would be efforts to extend its influence into the second session of the mandate Congress. It is perhaps equally unsurprising then that Democrats rose to argue against the idea of a mandate or for the idea that whatever mandate may have existed was now gone. We found four instances in which Democrats argued that the Reagan revolution was misread or had run out. Several Republicans also criticized the Reagan administration for holding too tightly to an expired mandate.

The mandate debate of 1996 opened with House Republican freshmen arguing that they still had a conservative mandate. However, several profiles of these freshmen provided evidence of the changing flow of political information from their constituents. One described how a Kansas Republican insulated herself by moving away from Speaker of the House Gingrich. A constituent volunteered a common theme in the media following the shutdown of the government. "This slash-and-burn attitude of the freshmen Republicans is terrible. They have misread the mandate" (*New York Times*, Jan. 14, 1996). Another first-term Republican from Kansas, Sam Brownback, received similar messages. A reporter captured the change this way: "If his election in 1994 seemed like a mandate, today it is much more difficult to get a sense of consensus among his constituents" (*New York Times*, Jan. 14, 1996).

Surely to the displeasure of many Republicans, the changing flow of information was exacerbated by a fellow partisan. In May 1996, Republican Senator Alfonse D'Amato visibly warned that Speaker Gingrich had misread the mandate of 1994 and was hurting the party's presidential candidate Senator Bob Dole. D'Amato's comments provoked a rebuttal by Republican House Leaders and generated stories of infighting within the GOP. The exchange produced a largely antimandate tone in the run-up to the presidential election.

If time and partisan wrangling erode the mandate consensus, the approach of the next election kills it entirely. Politicians and the media are both prospective out of necessity. Politicians must look forward to the next election to avoid defeat. The news media (almost by definition) must look to what is new and conflictual to retain readers and viewers. Table 6.1 shows that mandate coverage focusing on the upcoming election outpaces the past election in each of our three years. It is a shift in focus that naturally grows more acute as the year goes on. Figure 6.1 compares, by quarter, the proportion of mandate stories from 1982 and 1996 that cover the past (mandate) election and the forthcoming election. The shift in focus is clear. By the second quarter of the year, coverage of the upcoming election exceeds that of the previous one. The gap grows over the course of the year, with the new election dominating coverage as the voting approaches. The slow erosion of the consensus gives way to Election Day, whereupon we witness a new debate over what this new election means and how it instructs those in power.

Issues dominate the preelection discussion, some stories noting the possible referendum on the accomplishments of the mandated Congress, others focusing on the issues likely to constitute the content of any mandate that might soon be granted. The issues revolve around the major policy shifts we documented in previous chapters. In

Mandate Politics

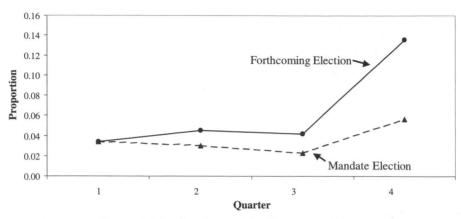

FIGURE 6.1. Quarterly Mandate Coverage in the *New York Times*, Comparing
Coverage Rates of the Previous and Forthcoming Elections, 1982 and 1996.

1966, the issue is white backlash against civil rights. In 1982, it is the
budget deficit and the need for tax increases. In 1996, a host of issues
were covered, but welfare reform is most prominent. In an impressive
nod to the power of the mandate consensus in the prior elections, the
upcoming election is framed by the major policy changes produced by
the mandate. The direct effect of the mandates we document may be
gone, but their indirect influence shapes electoral politics some two
years later.

6.2 THE SUBSEQUENT ELECTION

We began this book with a discussion of three elections, 1964, 1980,
and 1994, and how members of Congress reacted. To explore the final
influence of the mandates we look more closely at the subsequent elections: 1966, 1982, and 1996, and how members' mandate responses
affected their electoral fortunes. This closes the circle on the mandate
elections. We have already shown where mandate reactions originated
and how they altered the shape of American public policy. We now
want to demonstrate how they altered the choices of the voters two
years later.

  We approach this question through several steps. We begin by looking at a group that we have not yet discussed in great length, those members elected to their first term in the mandate election. These members

can serve as a unique barometer for public reactions. They were swept in during the supposed high tides that the mandates represented for their party. They also might be uniquely susceptible to the ebbs that came two years later. We then turn to the patterns of retirement. How members of Congress interpreted and reacted to the mandate two years earlier may change their decisions to stand for reelection. If so, we would be remiss to explore how voters reacted without first examining the choices they were offered. We finish by examining how the voters react to those members who did run in the subsequent election. We ask whether a member's reaction to the mandate affects whether or not he or she was successful in getting reelected and how it affected the member's margin of victory.

6.2.1   First-Term Members

Each of the three mandate elections saw a sizable number of new members of Congress elected. Across the three years, 237 members were elected to the House of Representatives for the first time. Of these, 183 (77 percent) were from the party supported by the mandate. The partisan surges bolstered already strong Democratic majorities in 1964 and more significantly altered the balance of power in 1980 and 1994. In 1980, the mandate surge gave the Republicans control of the Senate. In 1994, it gave the previously near permanent minority control of the entire Congress. The important role of the new members made them the focus on much mandate related media coverage. Many were elected in marginal seats, and were the obvious beneficiaries of the shifting public mood. The question then is how well they would fare absent the forces driving the mandate.

For better or for worse the new members were willing to face the voters absent the mandate. Nearly all chose to defend their seats. Five (9 percent) of the members from the disadvantaged party did not defend their seats two years later, and only fourteen (slightly less than 8 percent) of the mandate party members chose not to run – a small difference that is not meaningful. So, despite reason to suspect that voters might retreat from the mandate signal, most new members sought to keep their jobs.

The more interesting difference comes in their success in being reelected two years later. Only three new members from the party that suffered defeat in the mandate lost their seats two years later (a little more than 6 percent). In contrast, 53 of the 169 new members from the mandate party, nearly one-third, were defeated. This difference is striking. New members of the mandate party, after being swept in by national tides in their inaugural congressional victory, are quickly swept out by the move away from the mandate.[2] On the morning following the midterm election of 1982, a *New York Times* captured the results well, asking readers to "behold the pendulum now: it has swung very close to the center" (Nov. 4, 1982, p. A26).

Of course, these preliminary numbers may simply be a response to overarching national trends; the success and failure of these members may have little to do with the mandates and more to do with the standard surge and decline in congressional elections. We think the numbers are suggestive, but they clearly do not provide a test of how the congressional response to mandates influenced the electoral success of members in the subsequent elections. To get a better picture, we look at the full House and the fate of all of the members running for reelection.

6.2.2 Representation or Retaliation: Mandates Two Years Later

The electoral effect of the mandate reaction is a two-step question. First, we need to know how reacting to the mandate altered the decision making of the members themselves. The mandate reaction is rooted in a reading of voter intent and how that intent may influence the votes in the future. Members chose either to alter their roll call votes or not based upon a reading of political trends. Heading into the next election, voters can know, at least in principle, if a member responded by moving toward the mandate and will be able to judge him or her accordingly. They may choose to support the reaction by viewing it as an act of representation or they may punish the reaction as an act of overreaching.

Members of Congress also will have new information. They will surely have heard from some voters as to whether their reaction to the mandate was a good or a bad thing, and they will have new signals of changes in voter opinions. We thus have two avenues by which

---

[2] The best performance in this regard is the Republican freshmen of 1994, losing only 20 percent of their 1996 reelection bids.

the mandate can influence the next election. Members can use the information when deciding to seek reelection and voters can use it when deciding whether to reelect. We begin by asking whether a member's reaction to the mandate changes his or her decision to run for reelection. Second, we seek to uncover how the patterns of member response to the mandate two years earlier altered the decision making of the voters and, ultimately, the electoral fortunes of the members.

6.2.3   Retirements

The first question, then, centers on whether or not there is a relationship between reacting to the mandate and the decision to retire rather than seek reelection. Given how much the mandate consensus erodes in the second year of the mandated Congress, our expectations here are limited. That said, mandate reactions may be linked to retirement decisions for several reasons. The link should be strongest for the members of the losing party in the mandate year. The thrust of the mandate message was that their party was out of touch and their reaction was rooted in an effort to respond to voter movement away from their preferred position. If a member responds by changing his or her voting for a long period of time, this may lead a member to conclude that he or she is out of step with voters and at too much risk. However, no reaction might matter as well. Members who do not respond may see a risk in having shunned public opinion, be it real or socially constructed.

The incentive to retire is likely to be less strong for members of the party supported by the mandate. Their party was the beneficiary of the strong signal and they now have the benefits of incumbency and can portray themselves as representing what the voters asked for. Still, these members may be concerned with being seen as being too extreme, especially given the erosion of the message in the run-up to the new election.

Across the three years, 130 members retired before the following election (about 10 percent); 68 from the party advantaged by the mandate, 62 from the party that lost two years earlier. This is not a significant difference in the rate of retirement across the two parties. So, unlike the patterns among first-term representatives, the patterns for retirement are not a function of party. Falling on either side of the previous mandate does not appear to in and of itself induce greater perceptions of electoral risk. Which representatives retire after the mandate does not seem to depend on the broad national influence as the fate of the freshmen does. This is not a surprise given the shift in the media's tone regarding the mandate and the turning of attention to the forthcoming election. Party, however, is a crude measure of how the members experienced the mandate.

The more direct test of how the mandate influenced retirement decisions divides the members by whether or not they reacted to the mandate. Because the incentives for members and the effect of the mandate differ across parties, we first divide the members along party lines before dividing them based on whether or not they responded to the mandate. This allows us to compare the likelihood of retiring across whether or not the member reacted within each party.

Within the mandate party, there is no difference in the probability of retiring based on the member's reaction to the mandate. Overall, 10 percent of the members from the mandate party retired, and there is only about a 2 percent difference based on the members' reactions to the mandate. Of those who did not respond, 9 percent retired, whereas 11 percent of those who did react retired. This difference is substantively and statistically insignificant ($p > .20$). The members of the advantaged party do not appear to fear either the possibility of a general trend toward moderation or a more personal punishment for seeming too aggressive.

In contrast, there are differences for the disadvantaged party. Although the overall retirement rate for these members is not significantly higher than for the mandate party, this masks differences across whether or not the member reacted to the mandate. Just fewer than 10 percent of the members of the disadvantaged party who did *not* react to the mandate retired (a rate not significantly different from members of the mandate party who did not react). In contrast, over 15 percent of the members of the disadvantaged party who *did* react retired, a significantly higher rate of retirement than members of the same party who did not react. We thus have some evidence that members who, two years ago, perceived a strong enough shift in voter opinion to adjust their voting patterns may carry this view into the next election cycle. Those who reacted as if the mandate were a threat to their future prospects thus were more likely to bow out two years later rather than face a difficult reelection.

TABLE 6.2. *Predicting Representative Retirement, by Party (Logit Estimates, Retired = 1)*

	Disadvantaged Party Coefficient (Robust Standard Error)	Mandate Party Coefficient (Robust Standard Error)
Reacted to the Mandate (yes = 1)	0.53*	−0.09
	(0.15)	(0.54)
Seniority (Terms Served)	0.05*	0.02
	(0.01)	(0.03)
Loss in Victory Margin	0.99*	−0.11
	(0.49)	(0.25)
Gain in Victory Margin	0.83	−0.44
	(1.20)	(0.62)
Ideological Extremity (Folded ADA Rating)	−0.01*	−0.01*
	(0.00)[a]	(0.00)[b]
Previous Margin of Victory	0.16	0.57
	(0.79)	(0.42)
Year (1981)	−0.05	1.08*
	(0.11)	(0.17)
Year (1995)	0.25*	1.08*
	(0.05)	(0.17)
Intercept	−2.50	−2.89
	(0.23)	(0.42)
N	547	680

[a] Before rounding, the standard error is 0.004.
[b] Before rounding, the standard error is 0.003.
* $p < .05$.

These simple bivariate results are telling, but not conclusive. The results in Chapter 3 indicate that member reactions are related to factors that may also be related to the decision to retire, namely the member's margin of victory, his or her ideological extremity, and seniority. Thus, it is essential to account for these factors in explaining the link between reacting to the mandate and the member's decision to retire. We accomplish this through a simple logit model. The dependent variable is whether or not the member retired. The independent variables are the member's seniority, his or her ideological extremity (measured as the folded ADA score, the same as in Chapter 3), the member's margin of victory during the mandate election, two dummy variables for mandate year, and an indicator of whether or not the member reacted to the mandate. Table 6.2 presents the logit results for both the mandate and the disadvantaged parties.

Focus first on members of the disadvantaged party that suffered large losses two years earlier. For these members, how they interpreted the meaning of the previous election and reacted in their voting behavior altered their decision to seek reelection. Members of the disadvantaged party who reacted to the mandate were more likely to retire than those who did not. Converting the logit coefficient to the change in predicted probability shows that this effect is also substantively meaningful. With the other independent variables set to their medians, a member who reacted to the mandate is about 5 percent more likely to retire than one who did not. With fewer than 10 percent of the members retiring, this is a substantial increase. Notwithstanding the erosion of the mandate consensus, some members who saw a strong signal in the mandate election carried this signal forward and decided that they no longer fit a changed electorate.

Pinpointing electoral insecurity as the key, we see that it – measured as lost victory margin in the mandate election – also predicts the decision to retire. That completes the circle. We found in Chapter 3 that losing personal margin was a key explanation of changed member voting. Here we see that both the decision to change voting strategy and the decision to retire (when that change perhaps wasn't enough) follow from lost vote share. Members read the future from election returns. And the ones that matter most of all are their own.

Although we cannot know all the things a threatened member will know, it is clear that merely surviving in a year that is bad for the incumbent's party does not forecast electoral ease in the future. A close win makes it more likely that a member will be targeted by the other party in the future, more likely that he or she will face an attractive opponent, more likely that that opponent will be well funded. And if trends in the incumbent's vote share are in the "wrong" direction, then a decision to withdraw will often make sense. Retirement is better than defeat.

Seniority and ideological extremity also explain retirement decisions, but here our prior expectations are not strong. And with lost vote share in the model, the actual level of the previous margin of victory does not matter. Change is information with consequences. The level of previous security, in contrast, has none.

Turning to the mandate advantaged party (in the final column), we see evidence that almost nothing predicts the decision to seek reelection or retire. Apparently when a party is in ascendancy, retirements are more personal decisions. Of the predictors only ideological extremity passes a test of significance (barely) and it's coefficient (-0.006) is substantively trivial.

6.2.4   Election Results: Is Mandate Response Rewarded?

Although members take their knowledge about their constituents into account when they decide to retire, the retirement decision itself is not very informative about how voters react to their member of Congress' decision to respond to a mandate. To determine whether voters reward or punish a member's reaction to the mandate, we turn to examining the election outcomes themselves. We begin by looking at whether the member's reaction to the mandate influences his or her electoral success.

It is not entirely clear whether responding to the mandate should help or hurt a member's reelection. The influence depends on how voters see the mandate. If they see it as real, they would expect a representative to respond. If they do not see it as real, they might punish a member for moving away from the district's views. And there is a selection effect. If those who are most likely to change behaviors are those most threatened, then that threat itself predicts that they would not fare well in subsequent elections. So all things are not equal here. The threatened member may be an endangered species, no matter the response.

If voters reward members for being responsive and adapting to the perception of public opinion, we would expect that members who had stronger reactions to the mandate would be more successful two years later. This is especially true if we control for the messages they receive in the first place. That is, if a member received a message that his or her constituents had changed their preferences (as indicated by the election results in the mandate election) and the member did *not* react, then he or she should be less likely to win than a member who received the same electoral message and reacted to it.

Of course, if the mandates stem from a social construction of the meaning of the election and do not mark a true shift in the voters' preferences, then these same members may be disadvantaged. In this scenario, members are responding to phantoms, breaking from the delicate balance they had struck between their preferences and those of their constituents. It is plausible then, that we should see the opposite

reaction. Members who react to this incorrect message may pay a
penalty at the next election.[3]

We test for these opposing effects by first examining whether or
not the member is successful in his or her reelection efforts in the
election after the mandate. Our dependent variable in these analyses
is an indicator of being reelected (0 if the member loses, 1 if he or she
wins). The key independent variables are the indicator of whether or
not the member reacted to the mandate, and the measure of the number
of days that this reaction lasted.

The models also control for seniority, ideological extremity, the margin of victory in the mandate election, and the previous change in the
victory margin, again separated into gains and losses in order to separately examine the influence of experiencing a growing or shrinking
electoral margin. We examine only incumbents running for reelection,
and we again separate the analysis by party (pro- vs. antimandate).

Table 6.3 presents the results of the logit models for the mandate
and antimandate parties. Whether a member reacts to the mandate influences his or her reelection chances, but only for the disadvantaged
party. As shown in the first column, reacting to the mandate makes
a member of the disadvantaged party significantly more likely to be
reelected, though the length of this reaction is unrelated to reelection.
This is true even after controlling for their most recent electoral experiences. None of the variables tapping the prior margin of victory
is significant for the disadvantaged party. The effect of the mandate
reaction is relatively small, but nontrivial. The predicted difference in
the probability of being reelected between a member who reacts and
one who does not is .04. Thus, it seems that voters do modestly reward
members of the out party who capitulated to the mandate claims.

---

[3] This problem could be especially acute for members of the losing party. Reacting would
normally mean moderating, moving away from their party base to a more centrist
position. Such a reaction could then expose them to electoral danger within their own
party's primary, a challenge from someone who takes the pure party position. We
have investigated this prospect for 1982 and 1996 and found no evidence that reacting
members were more likely to face a primary challenge or that they did less well in the
subsequent primary if they did have one. Surely the fact that all reactions are temporary
is a big part of the explanation. Straying from the party line for a month or two or
three and then returning, long before a potential challenge could materialize, looks
like a prudent course for a member hedging against an unknown electoral future.

TABLE 6.3. *Election Results in the Subsequent Election, by Party (Logit Estimates, Victory = 1)*

	Disadvantaged Party Coefficient (Robust Standard Error)	Mandate Party Coefficient (Robust Standard Error)
Reacted to the Mandate (yes = 1)	1.23*	−0.38
	(0.60)	(0.45)
Length of the Mandate Reaction (Measured in Days)	−0.01	0.00[a]
	(0.01)	(0.00)[a]
Seniority (Number of Terms Served)	0.00[a]	0.02
	(0.05)	(0.04)
Loss in Victory Margin	−1.28	−0.11
	(1.18)	(0.77)
Gain in Victory Margin	−0.87	−1.13
	(1.01)	(0.82)
Ideological Extremity (Folded ADA Rating)	−0.01	0.03*
	(0.02)	(0.01)
Previous Margin of Victory	1.17	4.99*
	(0.97)	(1.10)
Year (1981)	−0.68	−0.75*
	(0.83)	(0.37)
Year (1995)	−1.38*	0.12
	(0.64)	(0.38)
Intercept	4.19	−0.42
	(1.10)	(0.44)
N	485	612

[a] Before rounding, the value is 0.003.
* $p < .05$.

Neither of the mandate reaction measures is significant for the mandate party. For these members, the previous margin of victory is the dominant predictor. Members with large margins of victory during the election are likely to be reelected. Ideological moderation is also a significant predictor, with more extreme members more likely to be reelected. Thus, we do not see the same penalty for advantaged party members – their reaction is unrelated to their chances of reelection the next election. Voters do not punish members of the mandate party. When acting under the mandate perception, conservatives can become more conservative and liberals more liberal without fear of reprisal.

TABLE 6.4. *Change in the Margin of Victory in the Subsequent Election, by Party*

	Disadvantaged Party Coefficient (Robust Standard Error)	Mandate Party Coefficient (Robust Standard Error)
Reacted to the Mandate	−0.01	0.06
(1 = yes, 0 = no)	(0.04)	(0.06)
Length of the Mandate Reaction	−0.0003	0.0002
(Measured in Days)	(0.0004)	(0.0004)
Seniority (Number of Terms Served)	0.01*	0.002
	(0.00)[a]	(0.003)
Loss in Victory Margin,	0.12	0.32*
Mandate Election	(0.09)	(0.11)
Gain in Victory Margin,	−0.05	−0.13
Mandate Election	(0.15)	(0.09)
Ideological Extremity	0.001	0.002
(Folded ADA Rating)	(0.001)	(0.001)
Previous Margin of Victory	−0.37*	−0.40*
	(0.07)	(0.06)
Year (1981)	0.03	0.02
	(0.05)	(0.06)
Year (1995)	−0.12*	−0.14*
	(0.03)	(0.04)
Intercept	0.29	0.11
	(0.05)	(0.05)
R^2	0.21	0.21
N	485	612

[a] Before rounding, the value is 0.003.
* $p < .05$.

Whether or not the member is reelected may be too broad a question. Of the 1,103 members who sought reelection in the three subsequent elections studied here, only 12 percent were defeated. To get a more nuanced understanding of how voters reacted to member behavior, we shift our attention from the simple question of win or lose to examining the member's change in the margin of victory. Again, we examine only members who ran for reelection, and look at the two parties separately.

The analyses of Table 6.4 show that how members reacted to the mandate does not influence the change in their victory margin. Neither the simple indicator of a reaction, nor the length of the member's reaction to the mandate, is related to the change in the member's margin of victory for either party. In the end, we have limited evidence that a mandate reaction matters two years later. Members of the disadvantaged party are more likely to win if they reacted, but their victory margins are unaffected. Based on these analyses, voters do not seem to be strongly influenced by how their representative reacted to the mandate.

6.2.5   Voters and Mandate Reactions

Our intention in this section was to uncover the electoral implications for a representative of reacting to mandate. Although there is not much of an effect, there are a few things worth mentioning. First, the choice of whether or not to respond does not seem to have any ramifications for members from the party advantaged by the mandate. It does not affect the likelihood of retiring or the reaction of the representative's constituents. For these members, the choice to become more extreme in their voting appears costless.

This is not true for the disadvantaged party. Members who capitulate to the mandate are both more likely to retire and less likely to be defeated if they do run for reelection. This is an odd combination. Members who react may see themselves as out of touch with voters and choose not to face them two years later. They would rather retire than try to explain their new positions to their constituents. If they do chose to run, however, moderating is successful – they are more likely to be reelected than if they did not moderate at the start of the session.

What does this mean for mandates, representation, and how voters want members of Congress to behave? The main implication is that members of Congress who are of the mandate party should follow along with the apparent change in the public's preferences. These members, who become more extreme in response to the mandate, are neither punished nor rewarded by voters. Given the choice, then, members should go along with the mandate (and their own ideology) and support more extreme policy. Members of the disadvantaged party, however, need to abide by the perceptions of the mandate. If they moderate, they cut their (admittedly small) chances of defeat considerably. In sum, voters reward moderation but do not punish extremism in reaction to the mandates.

The implication of these results is that members are seeing something that may be true. Disadvantaged members need to react to ensure their reelection. Advantaged partisans can support the new claims without fear of reprisal. This implies that the movement in opinion and votes that members of Congress see, and react to, may be real. If the mandate perceptions were ephemeral, we would expect the effects to be symmetric – punishing extremism while rewarding moderation. That is not the pattern. Instead, we see a clear electoral incentive, or at least the lack of a disincentive, for members to go along with the mandate claims.

We began with a theory that members of Congress would interpret a meaning in election results and, fearing for their futures, would alter their roll call votes. We have shown where the electoral interpretation comes from, which members of Congress react to these perceptions, and how these changes altered public policy. These final results suggest that members of Congress are correct in their reactions. Members who are threatened by the mandate are rewarded for reacting. Members who are emboldened are not punished. Thus, members react as if a mandate occurred. It appears that voters in the subsequent election act as if a mandate occurred as well.

7

Conclusion: A Mandate View of Normal American Politics

> ...You asked, do I feel free. Let me put it to you this way: I earned capital in the campaign, political capital, and now I intend to spend it.
> (President George W. Bush, Nov. 4, 2004, Post-Election News Conference)

Presidential elections in America always carry some suspense. Even when the outcome is pretty well foretold and the evening is just going to confirm confident prognostications, presidential elections are history-making events, their importance clear to all while they are going on.

7.1 THE 2004 MANDATE?

So it was on November 2, 2004. George W. Bush, seeking a second term in the White House, was leading in most of the polls. But the lead was not large and two polling organizations actually had Bush's opponent, John Kerry, ahead. So there was plenty of suspense on the election night telecasts.[1]

---

[1] That suspense was hyped by the afternoon leak on the internet of early – and it turns out, inaccurate – exit polls from the two key states of Florida and Ohio, showing Kerry with unexpected small leads. It was clear that an electoral college win for Bush required that he win both states. Thus, a Kerry lead in either, had it been accurate, was big news. Commentators stuck to the usual TV fiction that they did not know the exit poll results for states where the polls were still open, but it was obvious that they did know and so the actual Florida and Ohio results were contrary to the evening's script.

As the evening wore on Bush captured Florida – the site of the bitter 2000 recount – and by a margin larger than expected. And, with results coming in more slowly, he pulled out to a lead in Ohio, a lead that ultimately held up through confusion and controversy. The rest of the nation was so predictable that it was clear to electoral vote counters, amateur and professional alike, that Ohio was the game and that winning it was winning reelection.

As always happens, the win quickly translated itself into a tale of electoral blitzkrieg. A two and one-half point win, pretty much what would have been expected from the polls (and an unusually close victory for an incumbent seeking reelection), soon grew into a near-legendary win. Because of the surge in turnout in 2004 the close win actually gave Bush more popular votes than any previous presidential winner.[2] That total, combined with being the first president receiving the majority of the votes since 1988, was the basis for spinning 50.8 percent of the vote into a juggernaut victory, erasing, like a tsunami, all the familiar contours of American politics.

7.1.1   The Evidence of Election Night

As we have done for elections past, we can easily assemble the hard numbers known on election night to observe the facts commentators had to explain. Analysts looking for a Republican sweep would have seen a net change of four U.S. Senate seats, moderately large as these things go, but only one-third of the truly impressive 1980 showing.[3] The House win was the same, four seats, which counts as a smaller than normal turnover. And even the "win" was partly an illusion. All of the gained seats were from the state of Texas, the product of a recent and very controversial Republican reapportionment of the previous year, clearly not attributable to what was in the minds of voters on November 2. The GOP actually suffered a net loss outside of Texas. State governorships were a draw.[4]

---

[2] And those who were spinning the story would not point out that the loser, John Kerry, had the second highest vote total in American history, actually outpolling all previous winners. The point is not to praise Kerry's losing performance but to praise simple arithmetic; record turnout produces record vote totals.

[3] The net figure was the result of six Republican wins of previously Democratic seats minus two going in the other direction.

[4] Weeks later, after much recounting, Democrats actually claimed a gain in Washington State.

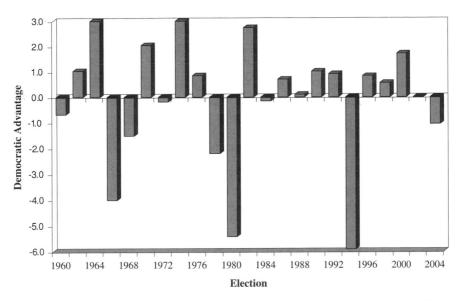

FIGURE 7.1. Cumulative Impact of Four Office Outcomes by Year: Repeated from Chapter 2 with 2004 Added.

As in Chapter 2 we standardize these net gains and losses by the normal experiences of other elections and put them all together into a single measure of the size of the Republican Election Day surge of 2004. Figure 7.1 has the great advantage of having been designed before the first vote was cast on November 2. So, unlike the statistical machinations of spin doctors designed to show that the Bush victory was huge – or trivial, depending on purpose – it was designed to put particular elections in the context of a half century's experience.

What is immediately obvious from Figure 7.1 is that, set in the context of other elections, 2004 tells a story of a mighty routine party win. Although election night always leads to excesses of imagination over facts, there just wasn't much story to tell of 2004.

What we call election night commentary was actually morning after commentary in 2004. Because the status of Ohio was contested until the early hours of Wednesday, November 3, the usual rhetoric was contained on election night and began in earnest the next morning. Vice President Cheney appeared on all major TV outlets with the mandate claim, "President Bush ran forthrightly on a clear agenda for this nation's future. And the nation responded by giving him a mandate."

Not surprisingly, the Democratic contender, John Kerry, saw less message in the outcome: "It's no small task taking on a sitting president, nor should it be. But I think the results show there was no overwhelming mandate" (John Kerry, ABC *World News Tonight with Peter Jennings*, Nov. 3, 2004).

When the candidates and party spokespeople disagree, we expect commentators to be similarly divided. They were:

Well, he won it fair and square, and it's a real victory as opposed to 2000. The margins may have been small this time but the margins all went in the president's direction. I don't think the president has a mandate. I think the divisions remain in the country over things like Iraq, over things like health care, over things like Social Security.... I think divisions are real and they're deep. (Richard Reeves, CBS, *60 Minutes*, Nov. 3, 2004)

And, ... as they bask in the glow here of a victory after a hard-fought campaign and a long Election Night, the White House was very quick to come out today to say they take this vote as a mandate for President Bush and his agenda, and they say that he plans to move aggressively ahead on that in a new term. In fact, in one of the congratulatory phone calls he was making to a fellow Republican, he said, "Now is the time to get it done." The president broadly laid out what his agenda for a second four years is going to be. (John Roberts, *CBS News Special Report*, 3:01 AM EST)

... even many Democrats tonight begrudgingly concede the right to claim for a second term a mandate. (John King, CNN *Newsnight with Aaron Brown*, Nov. 3, 2004)

Well, ... nobody has done it since 1988. The president wins reelection with a majority of the vote. It is a mandate. What will he do with it now? (Tucker Carlson, CNN *Crossfire*, Nov. 3, 2004)

Frankly, ... talk of mandate, whenever it was used, and I remember with only a plurality, president Clinton, ... talked about a mandate. The fact is, we elect a president who has an agenda. In this case, he has a powerful assembly of Republicans controlling both Houses in Congress. I think the mandate is overstated. But this president obviously will have a significant opportunity to drive forward his agenda. Again, that mandate thing always makes me nervous. But perhaps it's just a matter of semantics. What we do have is a – definitely a Republican-led government. And a president in a second term who will be focused as well as anything else on his legacy for the next four years. (Lou Dobbs, CNN *Judy Woodruff's Inside Politics*, Nov. 3, 2004)

Spin and counterspin, the mixed messages of election commentary, do not produce consensus, as we have seen for all previous cases. Response of professional politicians to mandate claims requires that losers join in the mandate talk. That did not happen in 2004 and George Bush's declining influence in 2005 reflected that fact.

We turn now to asking what we can learn about elections like 2004, normal elections in which the politics that ensue do not respond to mandate claims.

7.2 THINKING ABOUT NORMAL

In chapter after chapter, we have written about the abnormal cases of elections. We have not had much to say about the norm. But our results are informative about the many elections in the United States that do not produce mandates – although all presidential elections produce claims. And they are informative about the Congresses and presidencies that act on public policy absent a clear signal that the voters have spoken.

Here in this concluding chapter we shift focus back to the normal. We ask the question, "How much of what we think is normal in political life is really only the legacy of these three cases?" Our intent is to remove the evidence of these cases from theories about the norm so that the inferences we draw about what elections mean and how politicians respond to them do not rest on confusing the usual with the unusual.

Scholars often write phrases such as, "Take 1980, for example, ... " and then proceed to tell a story of how politics works normally from a case we now know to be abnormal. Our intention here is to remove some of the gloss on our understanding that arises from using these cases of swift and deliberate response to build a case for the normal functioning of American democracy.

7.3 THE EFFICIENCY OF DEMOCRACY

It is desirable in a democracy that, within limits, it be responsive to the changing will of the electorate. We would like a system in which an emerging majority of the public can transmit its views on the public order to government and see them reflected in alterations to public policy. The textbook view of American politics holds that this doesn't work very well. Majorities, that is, are frustrated again and again by veto players, those with the power to block action – in Krehbiel's (1998) terms by gridlock. Majorities in Congress cannot legislate because the constitutional system advantages those who wish to block change over those who wish to effect it.

The consequence is that it normally takes supermajorities to effect noticeable change. "Mere" majorities might get part way through the process, holding hearings, maybe passing something in one house, but then are stymied by the inability to overcome filibusters or force the hand of a reluctant White House. The usual outcome will be small change, altering public policy at the margins, often despite public approval of larger shifts. Majority failure in Washington has to mean failure also in representation, that a majority of the public lacks power to enforce its will. This can be overcome by supermajorities in the public and in government, but this is inefficient. It defeats the majority rule principle of democracy. Supermajority rule is a lesser thing. Action only when consensus is achieved delays the democratic linkage at best. At worst it utterly defeats it. We have learned from experience and from theory (Krehbiel 1998) that the supermajority requirement is not constant and not inevitable, that there are times when determined majorities rule. We have recounted stories in this book of majorities in 1965, in 1981, and in 1995 that captured the moment and swept aside delay and opposition as if it were easy and normal. It is obvious that it can be done.

But it is not at all obvious that it can be done without the good fortune of a preceding mandate election. The Great Society of 1965, The Reagan revolution of 1981, and the Contract with America of 1995 happened because people in Washington genuinely believed that voters were demanding change. This belief swept aside the usual minority power to block and to slow. Indeed, in the 1981 case, it swept aside the power of a *majority* party in the House to block the Reagan initiatives.

We have said all this before. Our point here is that absent a mandate we are impressed that gridlock is virtually insurmountable. Our three unusual episodes explain the most dramatic lawmaking of the latter half of the twentieth century. Without these few months, three or four or five in each of our three years, the history of legislation for the rest of five decades is one of almost unbroken gridlock. Absent perceptions of mandate, majorities have been frustrated and democracy is inefficient.[5]

7.3.1 The Underappreciated Status Quo

Why, we ask, are mandates so key to overcoming inertia? The beginning of an understanding is to note the normal safety of defending the status quo. Wise politicians understand that there is safety in current policy. That is so because current policy is not some historical accident (as is often claimed in debate) but instead the outcome of this very same process at an earlier time. If the political process were efficient (and surely it is not) then, absent changing circumstances, current policy would be politically optimal. It would please more citizens than any alternative.

So current policy, the status quo, will nearly always be, if not optimal, at least good enough that there is safety in its defense. It has been tested by previous political conflict and it has prevailed. Change carries dangers, some anticipated, some not. Members of Congress express this view in their voting strategies. Many will say, "When in doubt, vote no." If change is being proposed, that is, you want to be pretty sure what shape it will eventually take. Without such confidence, there is more electoral security in resisting than in advancing it. So it is normally difficult to defeat the status quo. Certainly, changing the composition of government, swapping some members of Congress of one party for members from the other will produce some change in public policy. It will move the median ideological position and the key veto points and alter the course of legislation. These changes, however, will be small – changes in the margins of government will produce only marginal changes in the status quo. Moreover, change in normal years, big or small, will be subject to the influences of log-rolling, lobbying,

---

[5] Numbers clearly are not enough. Even the 89th Congress, in which Democrats held effective supermajorities in both bodies, turned balky on Lyndon Johnson after the first few months of 1965. In early 1965, important legislation was crafted in the White House, passed in committee and on the floor, almost unchanged, by unified Democratic forces. Liberal Democrats had the power to legislate without compromise and without Republican support. By 1966, the same Congress reasserted the congressional prerogative, demanded to be convinced, and resisted much of what the White House wanted. Conservative Democrats joined with Republicans, as they had so often before, to say no to Lyndon Johnson.

and bureaucratic influence that often move policy away from public opinion and toward the status quo powers that be.

The mandate signal rises to importance because it directly confronts the status quo. When politicians perceive mandates, part of that is the perception that voters are sending a message that they will not tolerate the status quo. They have seen it and voted "no." Something else is called for. In this unusual situation change, sometimes *any* change, comes to seem electorally wise. If the voters find that something is broken, it is wiser to be on the side of fixing than on the side of defending the broken. This is an uncommon circumstance, to be sure, but when it occurs, it becomes shrewd politics to be identified as an agent of change.

In this circumstance, when cautious politicians are searching for an alternative to the status quo, simple majorities can legislate and democracy becomes, briefly, an efficient mechanism for translating citizen preferences into law. We should not expect to see such efficiency in normal times. Only when politicians believe that the status quo is unacceptable to voters will they enact wholesale changes in it. We end up being more pessimistic than Krehbiel, agreeing with him that there are circumstances under which simple majorities rule, but finding most instances associated with a mandate signal – and therefore unlikely without one.

7.4   DRAMATIC BEGINNINGS

A staple of American political lore, the idea of the presidential honeymoon is that there is a brief window for new presidents in which the force of the people's voice gives them power to rearrange the shape of Washington. More than just heightened public approval for the president himself, there is a sense that recent election conveys power to move – a power presidents find difficult to assemble at other times in their terms.

Historians like to write of a first 100 days in which the life of politics is imbued with some special force, when the normal barriers to attention and action are swept aside. Clearly time itself is part of the equation. When voters have spoken recently, their voice is more readily heard.

But is the recency of an electoral message enough? We think it is not, that the honeymoon idea is not generally applicable but is instead disproportionately influenced by a few special cases such as Lyndon Johnson in 1965 and Ronald Reagan in 1981. In those cases, the perception of mandate *and* recency of the message gave presidents the power to act.

Absent a perception of mandate, presidential frustration during the supposed honeymoon is common. A Congress controlled by his own party gave Bill Clinton grief over key appointments to his administration – it took three tries to get an Attorney General the Senate would confirm – and unceremoniously nixed his first proposal to permit gays to serve in the military. Both Presidents Bush experienced frustration and opposition in their early days in the White House. John F. Kennedy and Richard Nixon alike found that their proposals would not move Congress in the early going, both shaping their proposals to what could pass instead of shaping Congress to what they wanted.

What we conclude, in the end, is that pure honeymoons are much overrated. Take away the Johnson and Reagan cases (and of course the unstudied original first 100 days of FDR), in which presidents had the power of mandates and you have not much left. For most presidents, the first one hundred days constitutes a time marker for early press appraisals of the new administration, and nothing else.

New presidents do, on average, have better public approval than they will later experience.[6] But that has a simple explanation – that they haven't yet done anything controversial, made any mistakes, or suffered disasters on their watch – that seems sufficient.

7.5 ELECTIONS IN AMERICA: A REINTERPRETATION

From the very beginning of this project we have been guided by the rational expectations perspective. Originating in our sister discipline of economics, this notion is becoming an important building block of theories of politics as well.[7]

We get more explicit about the perspective here and then use it to put elections in context, to tell a story of how elections function in the signaling process between electorate and government.

---

[6] The "on average" qualifier is important. Since about 1980, the approval honeymoon seems to have faded away.

[7] See, for example, Alesina and Rosenthal (1995) and Erikson, MacKuen, and Stimson (2002).

7.5.1   The Rational Expectations Perspective

Rational expectations holds that individual decision makers act on all of the information they hold. From that basic assumption, that rational actors do not waste information, all else flows. Importantly, that means that expectations – information about the future – are in that class of information that is fully exploited. This radically alters our notion of how information drives action. In the rational expectations world people act on information when they receive it. Thus behavior anticipates facts predicted to happen in the future; the response to predicted outcomes precedes those outcomes; it does not follow them.

If people act on expectations about the future now, in the present, that means that markets will anticipate the outcomes. If those outcomes occur as predicted, then they will produce no further response when they occur. Every outcome can be decomposed into two portions, what was expected to occur in advance and surprise, the difference between expectation and outcome. In rational expectations, *only surprise is real information* and only real information produces response.

Our view of elections, to turn to politics, is that actors have expectations over outcomes – and professional politicians have well informed expectations. So politicians would be expected to act on expected outcomes before they occur, for example to reposition in advance of a coming election that will signal a change in the public's view. Thus, to the extent that expectations are accurate, actual election outcomes carry no novel information about the world and should produce no response.

But expectations are not always accurate. Professionals are highly motivated to get it right and, because the survivors are all successful, we expect them to be good at their vocation. But uncertainty about the future is inherent. The best informed expectations will sometimes be wrong. Thus surprises will occur; sometimes elections will turn out differently than highly informed observers expected in advance. These surprises are real information and real information will produce a response.

Elections change outcomes in two ways. The more obvious, the focus of nearly all election analysis, is that they change personnel. Some candidates win and some lose, altering the composition of government, and thus its choices. But second, elections sometimes signal an important change in public opinion, and that signal alters the behavior of those continuing in office (as well as the newly elected).

Our focus on changing in personnel is justified for some elections. When we elect presidents, for example, what mainly matters is that one party gets control of the apparatus of government and the other does not. The "message" of the election matters, but probably not as much as the fact of control. So, too, in the rare election that changes party control of a chamber of Congress, it is the change in personnel that is the dominant effect.

But the normal congressional election produces net party shifts of the order of 1 or 2 percent, leaving control undisturbed. In these cases, it is the "message" of election results – or more likely the absence of message – which is the more decisive piece of election effects. Because we too quickly reached the conclusion that elections are free of messages from the electorate in the early days of voting research, political science has been slow to understand the significance of the signal. That is, of course, the central point of this book.

What we now know is that elections do provide real information about public sentiment but that *it is not the results themselves, but only that portion that is a surprise, that matters.* When elections turn out as expected, for example the Nixon and Reagan reelection landslides, they signal nothing. It is the shocks, the stunning House Democratic wins of 1964, the big Reagan win and the twelve Senate seats changing from Democratic to Republican in 1980, and the massive GOP House wins of 1994, that produce a changed atmosphere in Washington.

What we can say about signals in elections yet to come is this: forget the result, that is not the thing that matters. Watch for the surprise.

We conclude by using our results to inform the normative implications of mandates.

7.6 THE DEMOCRATIC DILEMMA OF MANDATES

Over a decade ago, Robert Dahl (1990) put forward the idea that the presidency is a broken institution, long divorced from its original formulation. A leading contributor to an American democracy rife with conflict, it is driven by unchecked elites, and too often stalled in gridlock. The damage is a result of what Dahl refers to as the "pseudodemocratization" of the presidency, an institution with increasing links to the electorate, but subject to little real popular control. The democratization is evidenced by the president's rise to the position of a national party leader, the role of primaries in the nominating process, the willingness of the president to try to shape public opinion, and the regular claim of a mandate. The result is a presidency that uses rhetoric and executive powers to manipulate public opinion and to (excessively) influence Congress. The dilemma is that this more democratic presidency has significantly weakened the ability of Congress, the governing body most closely linked to the people, to oversee the president and to direct policy debates. Dahl in the end sees a system with less public consideration of candidates and less review of elites by their peers.

The mandate "myth" is but one element of Dahl's critique, but it is a myth so rooted in American politics that even alone, he believes, it raises significant problems for a representative democracy. He believes that the classic mandate theory has increased presidential power by portraying the president as the only representative of national interests, whereas Congress is portrayed as representing narrow special interests. The mandate claim has emboldened the presidency and brought increased conflict with Congress. This conflict has eroded meaningful deliberation, almost eliminated constructive compromise, and resulted in gridlock. For Dahl, the damage is made worse by the fact that all mandate claims are made of myths, not true public support, and are used to support deceptive and misleading interpretations of elections that harm the publics' understanding of public affairs.

If we accept Dahl's view, we are left with a presidency that uses mandate claims to dominate Congress and public policy. Such claims are not meaningfully contested nor do they erode with time. The claims, driven by the president's ability to go public, dominate electoral interpretation and hinder the development of a diverse interpretation of the meaning of an election.

The subsequent literature on mandates does little to dispense with Dahl's concerns. Current understanding largely shares Dahl's view that mandates are indeed mythical. Moreover, it supports the notion that presidents regularly claim mandates and work to foster the perception that they exist. Whereas Jones (1999) and Conley (2001) have advanced our understanding by exploring the strategic use of mandate claims and of the ability of Congress to fight them, mandate claims emerge from most elections and scholars continue to see them as presidential tools, often in support of misperceptions.

But what if mandates represent something else? If mandate claims are not as ubiquitous or as accepted as once thought, do they still pose a problem for the operation of a representative democracy? Or can we break from the myth of the mandate and its linkage to presidential claims to offer both a better theory and a view of the role of mandates in postelection politics that does not pose a dilemma for American democracy?

7.6.1 Normative Concern Squared with Empirical Evidence

We now are in a position to address normative concerns about the role of mandates. Underneath the normative debate lie empirical assertions about how mandates emerge and how they alter politics. We know about these things. What we know makes us less concerned than Dahl and others.

We know, to begin, that although mandate claims regularly emanate from the presidency, most of the phenomenon we have observed in these pages is not presidential. There are no "presidential mandates." The idea of a personal mandate associated with a personal electoral success finds no support in our data. The mandates we have seen originated from party sweeps and were interpreted as support for the party's core ideology. Personal success absent a party sweep – consider Nixon, 1972, Reagan, 1984, or Clinton, 1996 – produces nothing.

Partly this whole view – that mandates are accepted presidential interpretations of election wins – starts with a childlike conception of Congress. It is as if members of Congress wouldn't notice that the electorate had acted willfully unless the president told them. These are 535 ambitious, skilled, professional politicians engaged in a game in which the stake is their career. Each could serve as an expert commentator on election night, if not otherwise occupied with his or her own campaign. The idea that the size of a presidential win is a crucial signal of electoral intent ignores the fact that members and senators have much more compelling evidence, their own election result, in hand. When their own voters – people they know – change, they don't need a president to tell them something has happened. The fact that *we* don't pay much attention to the outcomes of individual congressional contests does not mean that they do not. And we mainly count up wins and losses, treating the voting totals as unwanted details. They know the margin they expected to see and how it differed from what they got. That discrepancy is a powerful signal, far beyond anything the president could do or say.

But what we have found that most dramatically eases normative concerns about presidents claiming mandates is that claims just don't matter. All presidents do it. And the evidence shows that mostly such claims fall on deaf ears. We have seen repeatedly that it is *consensus* on electoral message that carries force in Washington and moves politicians to rethink strategies. Consensus happens when both sides agree. Thus, the losing side need only deny electoral messages to keep the consensus from forming.

Political spin must work for some purposes and under some circumstances. Otherwise, why would professional politicians employ it so assiduously? Clearly it works best when not confronted with counterspin. But the social construction of an electoral mandate is an important matter. Unless opponents come to believe it themselves, we can count on the opposition to not allow it to go uncontested.

If mandates do not empower the president, and we believe they do not, then who do they benefit? In our view, the one player in politics most advantaged by mandates is the public. As we have noted, the checks and balances of our government are designed to prevent the will of the majority from becoming policy. The gridlock associated with normal politics stymies the desires of the majority. Because mandates seem to be the unique time when gridlock ceases and majorities get the policy they desire, their role may well to be enable responsiveness. As such, they are mechanisms of representation and force public policy to hew closer to the public's demands.

We are not predicating this on the assumption that the mandate is "real." It need not be a true signal of change for this to occur. If, however, it gets perceived as such, it greases the gears of government in such a way that brings public policy closer to the public's preferences. Voters may not have demanded such a change, but if members of Congress believe that they did, then the results are the same.

Of course, the efficient translation of public opinion into public policy may not necessarily be a good thing. The system of checks on policy making exists for a reason. The stymieing of demands of the public usually prevents the large scale changes in policy we see in mandate years.

The checks on public passions can help ensure deliberation, compromise, and, in some cases, consensus. Inefficient policy making can also ensure that Congress, acting on a mistaken belief, does not go too far.

Much of the Great Society was created under the rubric of the mandate of 1964. However, once normal politics resumed, the Great Society policies could not be overhauled until there were new mandates. Mandates may create dramatic swings in public policy, but the normal politics of gridlock hold these swings in place until the next mandate comes along. This can leave policy in place despite a changing public.

So, are mandates good or bad? It appears that the answer may be that they are simply necessary. The gridlock from normal politics holds public policy too stable; at least more stable than public opinion. Mandates, and the politics they create, seem to serve as important corrective mechanisms. In one short moment in time, they provide the changes in public policy for which demand had been building for years.

Bibliography

Alesina, Alberto, and Howard Rosenthal. 1995. *Partisan Politics, Divided Government, and the Economy*. Cambridge: Cambridge University Press.

Alesina, Alberto, John Londregan, and Howard Rosenthal. 1993. "A Model of the Political Economy of the United States." *The American Political Science Review* 87:12–33.

Alterman, Eric. 2003. *What Liberal Media: The Truth About Bias and the News*. New York: Basic Books.

Alvarez, R. Michael. 1997. *Information and Elections*. Ann Arbor: University of Michigan Press.

Arnold, R. Douglas. 1990. *The Logic of Congressional Action*. New Haven: Yale University Press.

Binder, Sarah A. 1996. "The Partisan Basis of Procedural Choice: Allocating Parliamentary Rights in the House, 1789–1991." *The American Political Science Review* 90:8–20.

Binder, Sarah A. 1997. *Minority Rights, Majority Rule: Partisanship and the Development of Congress*. Cambridge: Cambridge University Press.

Binder, Sarah A. 1999. "The Dynamics of Legislative Gridlock, 1947–96." *The American Political Science Review* 93:519–534.

Black, Duncan. 1958. *The Theory of Committees and Elections*. London: Cambridge University Press.

Campbell, Angus, Philip E. Converse, Warren E. Miller, and Donald E. Stokes. 1960. *The American Voter*. New York: Wiley.

Carmines, Edward G. and James A. Stimson. 1980. "The Two Faces of Issue Voting." *The American Political Science Review* 74:78–91.

Carmines, Edward G., and James A. Stimson. 1989. *Issue Evolution: Race and the Transformation of American Politics*. Princeton: Princeton University Press.

Caro, Robert A. 2002. *The Years of Lyndon Johnson: Master of the Senate*. New York: Vintage Books.

Congressional Quarterly Almanac. 1981. Washington: CQ Press.

Conley, Patricia Heidotting. 2001. *Presidential Mandates: How Elections Shape the National Agenda*. Chicago: University of Chicago Press.

Cox, Gary W., and Matthew D. McCubbins. 1993. *Legislative Leviathan: Party Government in the House*. Berkeley: University of California Press.

Cox, Gary W., and Matthew D. McCubbins. 1994. "Bonding, Structure, and the Stability of Political Parties: Party Government in the House." *Legislative Studies Quarterly* 19:215–231.

Dahl, Robert A. 1990. "Myth of the Presidential Mandate." *Political Science Quarterly* 105:355–372.

Davidson, Chandler. 1992. "The Voting Rights Act: A Brief History." In *Quiet Revolution in the South*, ed. Chandler Davidson and Bernard Grofman. Princeton: Princeton University Press.

Davidson, Chandler. 1994. "The Recent Evolution of Voting Rights Law Affecting Racial and Language Minorities." In *Controversies in Minority Voting*, ed. Bernard Grofman. Washington, DC: The Brookings Institution.

Edwards, George C. III. 1989. *At the Margins: Presidential Leadership of Congress*. New Haven: Yale University Press.

Erikson, Robert S. 1976. "Is There Such a Thing as a Safe Seat?" *Polity* 8:623–632.

Erikson, Robert S., Michael B. MacKuen, and James A. Stimson. 2002. *The Macro Polity*. New York: Cambridge University Press.

Fenno, Richard F. 1978. *Home Style: House Members in Their Districts*. Boston: Little, Brown.

Fenno, Richard F. 1991. *The Emergence of a Senate Leader: Pete Domenici and the Reagan Budget*. Washington: CQ Press.

Fiorina, Morris P. 1989. *Congress: Keystone to the Washington Establishment*. 2nd ed. New Haven: Yale University Press.

Groseclose, Timothy, Steven D. Levitt, and James M. Snyder. 1999. "Comparing Interest Group Scores Across Time and Chambers: Adjusted ADA Score for the U.S. Congress." *The American Political Science Review* 93:33–50.

Hershey, Marjorie Randon. 1992. "The Constructed Explanation: Interpreting Election Results in the 1984 Presidential Race." *Journal of Politics* 54:943–946.

Hill, Kim Quaile, and Patricia Hurley. 1999. "Dyadic Representation Reappraised." *The American Journal of Political Science* 43:109–137.

Jacob, Charles E. 1981. "The Congressional Elections." In *The Election of 1980*, ed. Gerald M. Pomper. Chatham, NJ: Chatham House Publishers.

Jacobson, Gary C. 1987. *The Politics of Congressional Elections*. Boston: Little, Brown.

Jones, Bryan D. 1994. *Reconceiving Decision-Making in Democratic Politics: Attention, Choice, and Public Policy*. Chicago: University of Chicago Press.

Jones, Charles O. 1999. *Separate but Equal Branches: Congress and the Presidency*. 2nd ed. New York: Chatham House Publishers.

Key, V. O. Jr. 1966. *The Responsible Electorate*. Cambridge, MA: Harvard University Press.

Kingdon, John W. 1981. *Congressmen's Voting Decisions.* 2nd ed. New York: Harper & Row.

Krehbiel, Kieth. 1998. *Pivotal Politics: A Theory of U.S. Lawmaking.* Chicago: University of Chicago Press.

Mann, Thomas E. 1978. *Unsafe at Any Margin: Interpreting Congressional Elections.* Washington, DC: American Enterprise Institute.

Markus, Gregory B., and Philip E. Converse. 1979. "A Dynamic Simultaneous Equation Model of Electoral Choice." *The American Political Science Review* 73:1055–1070.

Mayhew, David. 1991. *Divided We Govern: Party Control, Lawmaking, and Investigations, 1946–1990.* New Haven: Yale University Press.

Mayhew, David R. 1974. *Congress: The Electoral Connection.* New Haven: Yale University Press.

Mebane, Walter R. Jr. 2000. "Coordination, Moderation, and Institutional Balancing in American Presidential and House Elections." *The American Political Science Review* 94:37–58.

Miller, Warren E., and J. Merrill Shanks. 1996. *The New American Voter.* Cambridge, Mass.: Harvard University Press.

North, Douglass C. 1990. *Institutions, Institutional Change, and Economic Performance.* Cambridge: Cambridge University Press.

Page, Benjamin I., and Calvin C. Jones. 1979. "Reciprocal Effects of Policy Preference, Policy Loyalties, and the Vote." *The American Political Science Review* 73:1071–1089.

Pomper, Gerald M. 1981. "The Presidential Election." In *The Election of 1980,* ed. Gerald M. Pomper. Chatham, NJ: Chatham House Publishers.

Poole, Keith T., and Howard Rosenthal. 1997. *Congress: A Political-Economic History of Roll Call Voting.* New York: Oxford University Press.

Riker, William H. 1962. *The Theory of Political Coalitions.* New Haven: Yale University Press.

Schickler, Eric. 2000. "Institutional Change in the House of Representatives, 1867–1998: A Test of Partisan and Ideological Power Balance Models." *The American Political Science Review* 94:269–288.

Schickler, Eric. 2001. *Disjointed Pluralism.* Princeton: Princeton University Press.

Shugart, Matthew Soberg, and John M. Carey. 1992. *Presidents and Assemblies.* Cambridge: Cambridge University Press.

Stimson, James A. 1991. *Public Opinion in America: Moods, Cycles, and Swings.* Boulder, CO: Westview Press, 1991.

Stimson, James A. 1998. *Public Opinion in America: Moods, Cycles, and Swings.* 2nd ed. Boulder, CO: Westview Press, 1998.

Stimson, James A. 2004. *Tides of Consent: How Public Opinion Shapes American Politics.* New York and London: Cambridge University Press.

Stimson, James A., Michael B. MacKuen, and Robert S. Erikson. 1995. "Dynamic Representation." *The American Political Science Review* 89:543–565.

Stockman, David Alan. 1986. *The Triumph of Politics: How the Reagan Revolution Failed.* New York: Harper & Row.

Thomas, Dan B., and Larry R. Baas. 1996. "The Postelection Campaign: Competing Constructions of the Clinton Victory in 1992." *Journal of Politics* 58:309–311.

Weinbaum, Marvin G., and Dennis R. Judd. 1970. "In Search of the Mandated Congress." *Midwest Journal of Political Science* 14:276–302.

White, Theordore H. 1965. *The Making of the President 1964.* New York: Atheneum.

Wilcox, Clyde. 1995. *The Latest American Revolution?* New York: St. Martin's Press.

Wood, B. Dan, and Angela Hinton Andersson. 1998. "The Dynamics of Senatorial Representation, 1952–1991." *Journal of Politics* 60:705–736.

Wood, B. Dan, and Jeffery S. Peake. 1998. "The Dynamics of Foreign Policy Agenda Setting." *The American Political Science Review* 92:173–184.

Zaller, John R. 1998. "Monica Lewinsky's Contribution to Political Science." *PS: Politics and Political Science* 31:182–189.

Index